T 31927

2750

Photography and the Making
of the American West

Photography and the Making of the American West

Paul Clee

Linnet Books
North Haven, Connecticut

First published 2003 as a Linnet Book,
an imprint of The Shoe String Press, Inc.
2 Linsley St., North Haven, Connecticut 06473.
www.shoestringpress.com

Library of Congress Cataloging-in-Publication Data

Clee, Paul.
   Photography and the making of the American West / by Paul Clee.
      p.cm.
   Summary: Looks at the early history of photography in the United States, the
photographers who recorded life on the frontier, and how their vision and
artistry shaped public opinion about the West.
   Includes bibliographical references (p.) and index.
   Contents: Introduction: Picturing the West — Going West: the first wave —
Imagining America — War photographers and western journeys —
Photographers of the local scene — The many faces of the American Indian —
Saving shadows: the Indian photography of Edward S. Curtis — The last of the
great frontier photographers.
   ISBN 0-208-02512-X (alk. paper)
   1. Photography—West (U.S.)—History—Juvenile literature. 2.
Photographers—West (U.S.)—Juvenile literature. 3. West (U.S.)—Pictorial
works—Juvenile literature. [1. Photography—History—19th century. 2.
Photographers. 3. West (U.S.)—History—19th century.] I. Title.

TR23.6 .C54 2003
770'.978—dc21   2002030197

The paper in this publication meets the
minimum requirements of American National
Standard for Information Sciences—Permanence
of Paper for Printed Library Materials,
ANSI/NISO Z39.48-1992 (R1997). ∞

Designed by Dutton & Sherman
Printed in China by C & C Offset Printing Co., Ltd.

For my wife Violeta,
true partner in all things

Contents

ILLUSTRATIONS

ACKNOWLEDGMENTS

MANY THANKS TO my editor Diantha Thorpe for her guiding hand during the preparation of the manuscript. Aside from her merciless editing of the text, it was her vision that helped me to see beyond my first efforts to what this book could be.

INTRODUCTION

Picturing the West

THIS IS THE STORY of the first major historical movement to be recorded by photography—the exploration and settlement of the American West by non-native Americans. By the end of the American Civil War in 1865, photography was just emerging from its infancy. Much had been learned about field photography by the men who documented the war, but it was still a difficult craft mastered only with great effort and patience. But by the time the frontier was declared closed in 1890, George Eastman's Kodak cameras had put photography within reach of anyone who could push a button.

During the years between the end of the war and end of the frontier, the face of the West was changed forever: Railroads cut across the continent, the native people were exterminated or shunted onto reservations, and towns and cities sprouted on the Plains. The camera caught it all.

It started with a few hardy men who went west, most of them with exploratory expeditions, lugging their cumbersome equipment through uncharted country and working under nearly impossible conditions. By the 1880s, the corps of western photographers had swelled to a virtual army of around 15,000 operators.

No method for capturing a photographic image was available until 1839, so in many ways the development of photography and the exploration and settlement of the American West ran in parallel courses. Until the invention of commercial processing in the 1880s, photographers had to do it all themselves. It wasn't easy to make a good photograph even in a comfortable city gallery, as studios were called in the nineteenth century. It was ten times tougher if you had to pack and unpack a mule or two for every picture and work in all kinds of weather. Equipment was bulky and hard to handle. Cameras were big, about the size of shoeboxes or larger. And they were heavy, made of wood and metal–not exactly something you could slip into your shirt pocket or purse.

There was no such thing as film either. Each picture had to be taken on an individual plate. The plates varied in size, but 5" x 8", known as the "half plate," was the most common. For larger prints of the western landscape, big cameras were built to take plates up to 20"x 24". The earliest photographers used metal plates, but these were soon replaced by glass. You can imagine that a supply of enough plates to last several months would add quite a bit of weight to the photographer's equipment.

For another thing, just *taking* the picture presented its own set of problems. Exposure times were very slow. Modern films need to be exposed to light for only a tiny fraction of a second, unless you are photographing at night or in a closet. In the old days exposures had to be several minutes or more. That's why the camera had to be supported by a tripod; any movement would spoil the picture. A sudden gust of wind could shake the camera and blur the image, or the subject would move. The reason you don't see any action in very old photographs is that people had to remain motionless while the camera let in enough light to record them. If they moved, the image would blur, or not register at all.

Another difficulty was that there were no light meters to measure the amount of light available, so the photographer had to guess at how long to expose the plate based on conditions. Exposure on a bright, sunny day would be less than on a cloudy day. It took a lot of experience, trial and error, and guesswork to learn how to do this.

Taking the picture was only half the story. The plates had to be developed soon after they were taken, which meant that a darkroom–usually a black tent or small covered wagon–and chemicals and everything else had to be lugged out to the spot where the photographer was going to work. For the photographer in the Old West, this often required dragging everything up a mountain or through a canyon. That's why mules were a standard item of photographic equipment.

Considering these difficulties and the hardships and dangers of wilderness travel, you might wonder why the early photographers did it at all. There were several reasons. Part of it was simply the spirit of adventure and the challenge of doing something new, like climbing mountains or going to the moon. They were driven by the same kinds of ambitions that drew the pioneers westward. Most of the early frontier photographers earned their way as members of government-sponsored expeditions to explore the West. These jobs paid little or nothing, but they provided opportunities for travel into unexplored territory, and the photographers were usually allowed to sell their pictures privately.

Another reason was that easterners and Europeans were clamoring for photographs. There was a great deal of public curiosity about the mysterious land that lay beyond the Mississippi. Photography itself was a new and amazing invention. People were astonished and fascinated by the idea that reality could be recorded with such accuracy. Part of the fascination stemmed from the common belief that the camera didn't lie–that it showed things just as they were. Photographs were a kind of evidence that people and places really did exist exactly as they appeared. Photographs of exotic lands could turn a nice profit.

But the camera is more than a recording instrument, and during the second half of the nineteenth century, photographs played an important part in determining how people *perceived* the West–what kind of a place they imagined it to be. In the mid-1800s, when photographers first went west, the land lay under a blanket of mystery. What easterners knew of it came from the reports of travelers–often unreliable–and from rumors and tall tales. The boundaries and features of the land itself were vague. There were no accurate maps. Just to put *something* in their maps, cartographers often filled the vast blank spaces with names of places that were rumored to exist but were actually figments of someone's imagination.

One of the best examples of this sort of thing had to do with the search for a waterway connecting the Atlantic and Pacific oceans. The American continent had been an obstacle to traffic between Europe and Asia since the time of Columbus, who was on his way to India when he bumped into San Salvador in the Bahamas. Everyone—the Americans, the British, and the Spanish—was convinced that somewhere there existed a river spanning the continent east to west. The search was intense. It continued until the middle of the nineteenth century, with explorers traveling up and down every likely waterway. One prime candidate was the St. Lawrence River. Another was the Missouri. As Thomas Jefferson told Meriwether Lewis, the commander of the Lewis and Clark expedition, in 1803, "The object of your mission is single, the direct communication from sea to sea formed by the bed of the Missouri, and perhaps the Oregon. . . ."[1]

There was no transcontinental river. But the hope of finding one was so strong that mythical rivers flowed everywhere on eighteenth and nineteenth century maps, all based on nothing more than the flimsiest of rumors and dogged hope.

The fact is that the non-native people most familiar with the West were the least likely to publicize what they knew. They were the trappers and traders, mountain men like Jim Bridger and Jedediah Smith. But they didn't write about their travels and they didn't draw maps. Just the opposite, they tended to keep their knowledge of choice hunting grounds and good routes of travel to themselves. John C. Frémont, for example, thought he was the first white man to see the Great Salt Lake when he reached it in 1843. He was so thrilled by this that he wrote in his journal, "We felt pleasure also in remembering that we were the first who, in the traditional annals of the country, had visited the islands and broken with the sound of human voices, the long solitude of the place."[2]

What Frémont didn't know was that Jim Bridger and a band of

trappers had paddled around the lake in makeshift canoes almost twenty years before.

All of this uncertainty about the land only aroused greater curiosity, so when actual photographs filtered back to the eastern cities, people flocked to see them. And after glass plates replaced metal ones in the 1850s, making multiple prints possible, many photographers did a brisk business selling copies of their work. The technology to print photographs in magazines and newspapers wouldn't be invented until the end of the century, so the only way people could see them was by attending exhibits or buying copies for themselves. They did both in great numbers.

∼

WHEN PHOTOGRAPHY came on the scene in the mid-nineteenth century, Americans were divided and confused about both the land and its people. On the one hand was the idea of the West as the Great American Desert. This phrase was coined by Stephen Long of the U.S. Topographical Engineers in 1823. Long had traveled along the Platte River through what is now Nebraska and Colorado to the Rocky Mountains, then south and east through Oklahoma to Fort Smith, Arkansas. In his report he wrote, "I do not hesitate in giving the opinion that it is almost wholly unfit for cultivation, and of course, uninhabitable by a people depending upon agriculture for their subsistence."[3] On his map Long scrawled in large letters, GREAT AMERICAN DESERT!

This notion that the West consisted of nothing but a huge desert made its way into school geography books and maps. Estimates of its boundaries varied from one book to another, but they created a general impression that for a thousand miles, from the Missouri River to the Rocky Mountains, there was nothing but barren wasteland. Here is one example from a popular book called *A System of Modern Geography for Schools, Academies and Families* by Nathaniel G. Huntington. It is an account of what he calls Missouri Territory. Huntington wrote, "This territory is a vast wilderness, resembling a desert, extending from the state of Missouri and the river Mississippi, to the Rocky Mountains. It is a region of open elevated plains, generally destitute of forest trees, and interspersed with barren hills."[4]

Such books often compared this area to the Sahara Desert in Africa, giving the impression that the whole of the Great Plains was a country of drifting sand dunes. This impression was reinforced by the accounts of pioneers who had traveled overland to Oregon and California. In his book *The Oregon Trail* (1849), Francis Parkman described central Nebraska as a wasteland:

> Two lines of sand-hills, broken often into the wildest and most fantastic forms, flanked the valley at the distance of a mile or two on the right and left; while beyond them lay a barren, trackless waste—The Great American Desert—extending for hundreds of miles to the Arkansas on the one side, and the Missouri on the other. Before us and behind us, the level monotony of the plain was unbroken as far as the eye could reach. Sometimes it glared in the sun, an expanse of hot, bare sand; sometimes it was veiled by long coarse grass. Huge skulls and whitening bones of buffalo were scattered everywhere; the ground was tracked by myriads of them, and often covered with the circular indentations where the bulls had wallowed in the hot weather.

The image of the West as an arid, treeless desert prevailed until the Civil War. But with the end of the war the federal government, supported by leaders of business and industry, stepped up efforts to expand settlement beyond the Missouri River. The government sent out expeditions to map the country and report on its natural resources. Railroads pushed across the Plains. Increased settlement meant access to new resources and the creation of new markets for eastern industries. It also meant economic growth that would benefit landowners in the agricultural areas of eastern Kansas and Nebraska. But to attract more settlers, it was necessary to soften the hostile image of the Plains. The way to a new vision of the West can be found in the words of a

Missouri trader named Josiah Gregg, who published a book titled *Commerce of the Prairies* in 1844. In it he wrote,

> Why may we not suppose that the genial influences of civilization–that extensive cultivation of the earth–might contribute to the multiplication of showers, as it certainly does of fountains? Or that the shady groves, as they advance upon the prairies, may have some effect upon the seasons? At least, many old settlers maintain that the droughts are becoming less oppressive in the West. . . . May we not hope that these sterile regions might yet be thus revived and fertilized, and their surface covered one day by flourishing settlements to the Rocky Mountains?[5]

This idea was picked up by newspapermen covering the building of the Union Pacific Railroad through Kansas and Nebraska in 1867. They reported claims that as more people came into the country rainfall somehow increased. The mere act of settlement, they suggested, would cause more rainfall, which in turn would make agriculture–and therefore civilization–possible. Further weight was given this notion by Ferdinand Hayden, a medical doctor turned explorer and geologist who led several exploratory surveys of the West in the 1860s and 70s. Hayden thought that settlement and planting trees would result in a change in climate. As he put it,

> The settlement of the country and the increase of the timber has already changed for the better the climate of that portion of Nebraska lying along the Missouri, so that within the last twelve or fourteen years the rain has gradually increased in quantity and is more equally distributed through the year.[6]

The support of people like Hayden gave these theories an aura of scientific respectability. A popular slogan–"Rain follows the plow"–captured the spirit of this new vision. The transformation of the image of the West from desert to farmland reflected a recurring dream of white America–what historian Henry Nash Smith called "the Garden of the World." As Smith explains in his book *Virgin Land*,

With each surge of westward movement a new community came into being. These communities devoted themselves not to marching onward but to cultivating the earth. They plowed the virgin land and put in crops, and the great Interior Valley was transformed into a garden: for the imagination, the Garden of the World.[7]

As different as they were, the images of the desert and the garden had one thing in common: At the heart of each was the question of the land's usefulness. Would crops grow there? Could the land support towns and cities? Then in the mid-nineteenth century a third view began to gain favor. In a lecture given in 1851, Henry David Thoreau, who was to write *Walden* in 1854, made his famous declaration, "In Wildness is the preservation of the World." The idea that wilderness is valuable for its own sake found devoted followers, and the American conservation movement was born. Wild nature was revered as a source of spiritual and moral inspiration, an idea that became a powerful theme in American art and literature. It was believed that in unspoiled nature God made his presence in the world known.

In the same way as Americans' views of the land were both vague and divided, their attitudes toward its earliest inhabitant, the American Indian, were uncertain and often contradictory. Was the Indian the Noble Savage, as some thought, unspoiled by civilization and living as nature intended? Or was the Indian the Red Devil, savage and bloodthirsty, obstructing the progress of civilization? From the beginning of European contact, the North American continent was commonly described as empty–as if no one lived there at all. When the presence of the Indian was acknowledged, it was more often than not as a symbol or caricature, rather than as a real person.

Into this unstable brew of myth and reality walked the photographer, equipped to show the land as it really was–or so it was thought. Photography, with its ability to give an impression of factual truth, helped to fill in some of the blank spaces on the map, to give them a concrete reality. But while photographs gave the appearance of objectivity, they were also colored by the preconceptions and purposes of the men behind the camera. These were men of their time, and the way they pictured the West was bound to be shaped by commonly held ideas about nature, the land, the native people, and the destiny of the nation. What's more, much western photography in the nineteenth century was done on commission for the government or for private enterprise, so the needs of the client would affect the result. If an executive of the Union Pacific wanted to encourage tourism and settlement along the railroad line, for example, a photographer returning with pictures of a desolate wasteland or hostile savages would soon be looking for other work.

The *way* photographers approached the landscape and the people had a lot to do with *how* the blank spaces on the map were filled in, and in this way, photography played an important part in the transformation of the American West.

CHAPTER ONE

The First Photographs

THE PHOTOGRAPHS TAKEN by the earliest frontier photographers, during the 1850s, didn't look very much like the photographs we are used to seeing today. At that time, no good process had been invented for printing photographs on paper. Since these early photographs were made on thin sheets of copper, there was only one copy of each photo, and the picture was the size of the original plate. It could not be copied or enlarged.

These photographs were called *daguerreotypes*. They were named for their inventor, the Frenchman Louis Jacques Mandé Daguerre, who was the first person to figure out a way to render the image made by the camera permanent–what photographers call *fixing* the image.

Daguerre announced his invention in 1839, but knowledge of how a camera works had existed for many years before that. In the fifteenth century the Italian artist and inventor Leonardo da Vinci described how light passing through a tiny hole in one wall of a dark room will form an image of whatever is outside on the opposite wall. The image would be upside down and reversed from left to right, but clear in every detail. So the word "camera" comes from the Italian *camera obscura*, meaning "dark room."

By Daguerre's time the *camera obscura* had become a much more complex instrument than a box with a hole in it. It was fitted with a lens, which produced a much brighter and sharper image. Some *cam-*

eras obscura also contained a mirror that reflected the image up onto a piece of frosted glass called a *ground glass*. In this way, a piece of thin tracing paper could be laid over the image on the ground glass and the picture could be traced with a pencil. Daguerre simply inserted a sensitized copper plate in place of tracing paper.

In addition to an understanding of how a camera worked, it was also known well before Daguerre's time that many substances change when they are exposed to light.

In 1802 the British experimenter Thomas Wedgewood discovered that light darkens a piece of paper coated with a solution of silver nitrate. He experimented with this coated paper by first painting a picture on a piece of clear glass, then placing the glass on top of a piece of sensitized paper set out in the sun. Different parts of the painting allowed different amounts of light to pass through to the paper underneath. Where nothing was painted on the glass, a lot of light passed through. Where there was dark paint, little or no light passed through. The parts of the paper that received the most light turned dark, while the areas that received little or no light remained white or turned various shades of gray.

Wedgewood had produced what we now call a *negative*—dark and light areas come out opposite from those in the original scene. If you photograph a white flower against a dark wall, for instance, the negative will show a black flower against a white wall. Then if you make a print from the negative, what you get is a *positive*—everything back to normal.

Much to Wedgewood's disappointment, he could not find a way to prevent the picture from fading. The chemicals in the paper remained light sensitive, so continued exposure to light turned everything dark. Wedgewood couldn't fix the image, so he kept his pictures, which he called "sun prints," in a dark place only to look at them once in awhile by the dim light of a candle.

Even before Daguerre's announcement of his process in 1839, a number of experimenters had been working feverishly trying to find a way to make lasting photographic copies on paper. In England, Fox

Daguerrotype of a Peddler (ca. 1840-60) by Myers. This occupational portrait, with its relentless symmetry and the neck brace visible between the subject's legs, seems determined to remain "fixed" in more ways than one. Courtesy of the Library of Congress Prints and Photographs Division, repro. LC-USZC4-4161.

Talbot and Sir John Herschel worked out separately but simultaneously a method for fixing the image made by the *camera obscura* on sensitized paper. This was a negative image. As he worked on the problem, it occurred to Talbot that he could make a positive image from the negative by placing the negative on top of another piece of paper and shining light through it. He tried it, using the sun as his source of light. It worked.

Talbot named these pictures after himself, calling them "Talbotypes." The problem with them was that the positive print showed the texture of the paper used as a negative. Something better than paper was needed.

It was Sir John Herschel who hit upon the idea of coating glass with the light sensitive chemicals and using the glass plate as a negative. The idea worked, but the process was even slower and trickier than making a daguerreotype, and the plates required longer exposures in the camera. There was also a problem getting the light-sensitive material to stick to the glass.

The search for a substance that would stick to the glass covered everything from milk to egg whites–even the slime that snails leave behind as they glide along. Egg whites–albumen–worked pretty well, and some good photographs were made from negatives that used it. But this process also proved to be extremely slow. Exposures ran about three hours, and during that much time all kinds of bad things could happen. The camera could move, the subject could move, the weather could change.

It wasn't until 1851, when an Englishman named Scott Archer tried some stuff called *collodion*, that glass plates became practical. Collodion is a syrupy solution that dries to a tough, transparent film. It is used in medicine as an adhesive to cover wounds.

Archer saturated the collodion with light-sensitive chemicals and flowed it evenly over a glass plate. Collodion stuck to the glass, all right, but once again there was catch: The plate lost its sensitivity as it dried, so it had to be used wet. Not only that, but the plate also had to be

HOW DAGUERRE MADE HIS PICTURES

First, Daguerre took a thin sheet of copper, about 6" x 8", that was plated with a coat of silver. Then he polished it to a fine finish and washed it in an acid solution and heated it over a candle. Next, in a dark room he placed the plate over an opening in the lid of a box. In the bottom of the box was a solution of iodine. As the iodine evaporated, the fumes combined with the silver on the plate to form a compound called silver iodide. This compound is sensitive to light.

Daguerre then put the sensitized plate into the back of a *camera obscura* so that the image projected by the lens would fall on it. The *camera obscura* was aimed at the view to be photographed, the cap was removed from the lens, and the plate was exposed to light. It took anywhere from five to forty minutes for the lens to admit enough light to form an image on the plate. The amount of time depended on the brightness of the day.

After it had been exposed long enough, there was still no visible image on the plate. The plate had to be developed to bring it out. Daguerre developed his plate by placing it over a pan of mercury that was heated to 117 degrees F (62 degrees C). Vapors of the heated mercury rose and combined with the surface of the metal, slowly forming the picture.

Once the picture appeared, Daguerre washed the plate with water and a solvent that removed any remaining light-sensitive material. In this way the image was fixed.

developed while it was still wet—which meant that, as with the daguerreotype, the photographer had to lug everything out to the site. Even so, western photographers from the 1860s on favored glass plates because any number of copies could be made from them.

Like most inventions, photography rested on the work of many people. Daguerre's contribution was in finding a way to make the image permanent–fixing it. Until glass plates came along, the daguerreotype ruled photography. It was the process that all of the frontier photographers used in the earliest years of photography in the West, the 1850s.

Both the daguerreotype and the wet plate were complicated processes, and they tested the skill and determination of those who tried to use them. In those days a photographer had to have plenty of skill, knowledge, and patience to make a photograph. Not to mention a strong dose of luck. And remember that the frontier photographers had to do all of this in the field, often in bad weather and under dangerous conditions.

CHAPTER TWO

Going West
The First Wave

IN THE SPRING of 1853 an expedition left St. Paul, Minnesota, heading west. It was one of the parties sent out at that time to scout the best route for a railroad to the Pacific Ocean. The leader was Governor Isaac Stevens of Washington Territory. His task was to survey a possible northern route.

Accompanying Stevens on this expedition was an artist named J.M. Stanley. Before the age of the camera, it was common practice to take artists on these journeys of exploration to sketch the landscape, the people, the plants, and the animals. Stanley was a skilled artist. He had a solid reputation for his paintings of American Indians, but he had also learned another useful skill. He had mastered the new art of making daguerreotypes, and he took his equipment with him.

Unfortunately, as happened to many photographs from the 1850s, none of Stanley's daguerreotypes have survived. (Or at least none have been found yet.) We only know of them from notes in Governor Stevens's diary. For example, while the party was at Fort Benton on the Missouri River, Stevens wrote, "Mr. Stanley commenced taking Daguerreotypes of the Indians with his apparatus. They are delighted and astonished to see their likenesses produced by the direct action of the sun. They worship the sun, and they considered Mr. Stanley was inspired by their divinity, and he thus became in their eyes a great medicine man."[1]

Photographs are so common now that they have lost much of the feeling of magic that they once had. But especially to people who have never seen them, the ability to create a likeness by invisible means does seem magical. There are still plenty of people in the world today who don't like their pictures taken because they feel that photographs steal their soul or give power to the person who possesses them.

In the same year as the Stevens expedition, 1853, another daguerreotypist, Solomon Carvalho, went out with a party led by Col. John C. Frémont. They explored the country from Westport, Missouri, to what is now Utah. Carvalho was, like Stanley, first and foremost an artist. At one time he had made a living drawing charcoal portraits. Carvalho kept a detailed journal of the expedition, so we have more information about his work. But as happened to Stanley, almost all of his photographs have been lost. No one knows for sure what happened to them, but chances are they were destroyed in a fire at the Frémont house where they were being kept.

Like Stanley, Carvalho photographed Indian villages along the way, and like Stanley, he learned something about the "magic" of photography. In his account of the expedition, he described an experience among the Cheyenne: "I went into the village to take daguerreotype views of their lodges, and succeeded in obtaining likenesses of an Indian princess—a very aged woman, with a papoose, in a cradle or basket, and several of the chiefs, I had great difficulty in getting them to sit still, or even to submit to have themselves daguerreotyped. I made a picture, first, of their lodges, which I showed them. I then made one of the old woman and papoose. When they saw it, they thought I was a 'supernatural being;' and, before I left camp, they were satisfied I was more than human."[2]

Carvalho also amazed the Indians with the mercury (which is also called "quicksilver") that he brought to develop his plates. Applied to brass, mercury coats it and turns it silver. Carvalho wrote that after making the portrait of the Indian princess, he motioned for her to give him one of her bracelets. "She very reluctantly gave me one," he wrote.

"I wiped it very clean, and touched it with 'quicksilver.' It instantly became bright and glittering as polished silver. I then presented her with it. Her delight and astonishment knew no bounds. She slipped it over her arm, and danced about in ecstasy. As for me, she thought I was a great 'Magician'."[3]

After this, the Cheyenne pleaded with Carvalho to stay with them.

Carvalho's journal, *Incidents of Travel and Adventure in the Far West*, gives us a good picture of the conditions a photographer had to deal with in those days. He wrote that every time he wanted to take a picture all of his equipment had to be hauled to the site on the backs of mules. Sometimes they had to travel over rugged mountain terrain where there were no trails and certainly no roads. Since daguerreotypes had to be developed right away, he had to pack his cameras, tripod, darkroom tent, chemical trays and bottles, and various other paraphernalia. When he arrived at a good location, everything had to be unpacked and set up, the copper plate prepared, the picture taken and developed. If the exposure was wrong or the camera moved, it had to be done all over again. Then it all had to be packed back on the mules and the whole outfit moved to another spot.

"To make a daguerreotype view," Carvalho said, "generally occupied from one to two hours; the principal part of that time was spent in packing, and reloading the animals." [4]

When the Frémont party finally arrived at the Rocky Mountains, they faced some serious hardships. They crossed the mountains in the dead of winter in below-freezing weather and deep snow. Nevertheless, Carvalho insisted on photographing. In his journal he described one incident in which a difficult job became a spiritual experience:

> Near by our camp, a rugged mountain, barren of trees, and thickly covered with snow, reared its lofty head high in the blue vault above us. The approach to it was inaccessible by even our surefooted mules. From its summit, the surrounding country could be seen for hundreds of miles. Col. Frémont regretted that such important views as might be made from that point, should be lost, and gave up the idea as impracticable from its

dangerous character. I told him that if he would allow two men to assist me in carrying my apparatus up the mountain, I would attempt the ascent on foot, and make the pictures; he pointed out the difficulties, I insisted. He then told me if I was determined to go he would accompany me. . . .

After three hours' hard toil we reached the summit and beheld a panorama of unspeakable sublimity spread out before us; continuous chains of mountains reared their snowy peaks far away in the distance, while the Grand River plunging along in awful sublimity through its rocky bed, was seen for the first time. Above us the cerulean heaven, without a single cloud to mar its beauty, was sublime in its calmness.

Standing as it were in the vestibule of God's holy Temple, I forgot I was of this mundane sphere; the divine part of man elevated itself, undisturbed by the influences of the world. I looked from nature, up to nature's God, more chastened and purified than I ever felt before.[5]

Carvalho's experience is a perfect example of the experience of the *sublime* in nature. In the aesthetics of the late-eighteenth and nineteenth centuries, the sublime was the highest value, greater than the picturesque or the beautiful. What set the sublime apart was the feeling it aroused in the viewer of being overpowered by something, like the energy of a thundering waterfall or the size of a towering peak. Strong emotion, tinged with astonishment and even terror, was the essence of the sublime. This idea was intertwined with the romantic belief that God made his presence known in the world of majestic, unspoiled nature. It was a value sought in both nature and art, and was put forward as a reason to preserve wilderness. The West, which was full of impressive natural phenomena, became the place to go if you wanted to encounter the sublime.

Capturing the sublime on a photographic plate often meant enduring brutal hardships. In an 1855 letter to the editor of a magazine called *Photographic Art Journal*, Carvalho wrote, "I succeeded beyond my utmost expectation in producing good results and effects by the Daguerreotype process, on the summits of the highest peaks of the Rocky Mountains with the thermometer at times from 20 degrees to 30 degrees below zero, often standing to my waist in snow, buffing, coating, and mercurializing plates in the open air."[6]

Because of the terrible winter weather, the men of the expedition left much of their baggage behind in the mountains. It was so bad that one man died from exhaustion. They killed their horses for food. Carvalho had to abandon his daguerreotype equipment, but he managed to save the plates themselves. Although few of his photographs have survived, Carvalho later gained a reputation for his paintings of Rocky Mountain scenes. These paintings were probably based on his experiences with the Frémont expedition.

A few other explorations and surveys of the West were carried out during the 1850s. They included photographers, but little is known of what they did and none of their work remains. It would be a few years yet before photographs of western exploration would be preserved for future generations—for there was an interruption that cut off exploration for the next four years.

~

ON APRIL 12, 1861, Confederate troops fired on the Union garrison at Fort Sumter in Charleston, South Carolina. This attack touched off the American Civil War and put a temporary end to government expeditions and thus to most photography between the Missouri River and the Rocky Mountains. But west of the Rockies, in California, independent photographers were introducing the world to the beauties of the Far West.

San Francisco in the 1860s was a thriving metropolis, the only big city west of St. Louis, Missouri. It became an early center for western photography. The city itself, in its picturesque setting, drew the attention of photographers. But San Francisco was also within striking distance of the wild beauties of the Sierra Nevada mountains, and it was here that California photographers accomplished their finest work. The best of them was Carleton Watkins. He became a photographer almost by accident.

Watkins was born in 1829 in Oneonta, New York. He made his way to California around the time that gold was discovered at Sutter's Mill in January, 1848. It seems that he wasn't one of those who struck it rich, though, for in 1855 he was working as a clerk in a store in San Francisco when opportunity knocked. One day a friend of his, a daguerreotypist named R.H. Vance, rushed into the store and begged Watkins to help him out in an emergency. Vance owned several daguerreotype galleries in the area. It so happened that the man who had been running his gallery in San José had suddenly quit and Vance needed someone to manage things until he could find another photographer. Watkins admitted that he didn't know the first thing about photography, but Vance said he just needed someone he could trust to look after things for a while.

So Watkins accepted the offer—a decision that changed his life.

Vance showed him the ropes, and Watkins learned his craft quickly. He was a natural. He soon opened his own gallery in San Francisco and made his living mostly doing portraits. But it soon became clear that his best work was in landscape photography. He loved the outdoors and he loved photography, so it was a perfect match. He became famous for his pictures of California's giant redwood trees and the natural wonders of Yosemite Valley.

In his landscapes, Watkins abandoned the daguerreotype in favor of the wet-plate process, which made multiple copies possible. He began photographing in Yosemite in 1861. To capture a sense of the magnificence of the scenery, he wanted to make larger pictures than the available glass-plate cameras would allow. But at that time there was no good way of enlarging photographs.

To enlarge a photograph, you need a projector of some kind, similar to a slide or movie projector. In Watkins's time there were no electric lights, and although there had been experiments with enlargers that used the sun for illumination, the results were pretty poor. So Watkins designed a giant camera, big enough to take a plate 18" x 22". Large cameras like this became known as *mammoth-plate* cameras. The big plate made the process even more difficult. It took consider-

Yosemite Valley from the Best General View (ca. 1866) by Carleton Watkins. Here Watkins captured in one photograph the most spectacular features of Yosemite Valley: Cathedral Rock, Half Dome, El Capitan, and Bridalveil Falls. Clouds were added from another negative. Courtesy of the Library of Congress Prints and Photographs Division, repro. LC-USZ62-17947.

able skill to get the collodion to flow evenly on the glass, and once that was done the plate still had to be sensitized and then exposed and developed while wet. What's more, at that time Yosemite was not a national park with well-groomed trails and tidy campgrounds. It was a wilderness. Watkins needed twelve mules, five just for photographic equipment and the rest for food, shelter, and camping gear.

Watkins wasn't the only one photographing in Yosemite during the 1860s and 70s. There were many others, including C.L. Weed and Eadweard Muybridge, and since then legions of photographers have turned their lenses toward Yosemite Falls and El Capitan. Pictures of Yosemite's natural wonders drew admiring crowds in the East and abroad, and the valley quickly became the supreme symbol of God's Garden, the American Eden. But even today, Watkins's photographs are among the best ever made. In his beautifully framed views, nature appears at its quiet, unspoiled best, setting the tone for a continuing tradition in landscape photography.

Carleton Watkins soon became one of the leading photographers in the country, if not the world. His photographs helped convince Abraham Lincoln to sign the Yosemite Bill in 1864, protecting the valley from exploitation. Along with similar work by other photographers, his pictures helped to draw eastern tourists to the West, especially after the completion of the transcontinental railroad in 1869. His photographs sold well, and in 1871 Watkins built the Yosemite Art Gallery to display and sell his work. It was one of the largest galleries in the world at that time.

Watkins's photographs provided proof of the enormity and magnificence of the western landscape. Reports about the West that reached people in the East often sounded like exaggerated tales of a legendary land: huge trees, towering mountains, endless deserts. That's one reason why Watkins needed a big camera: It had to do justice to the size of the country he was photographing. When his pictures were shown in the East, people had to admit that the tall tales of wide-eyed travelers might not be so "tall" after all.

Yo Semite Falls. 2630 ft. (stereograph, glass, 1861, 6.03 x 13.2 cm) by Carleton Watkins. In this stereograph, the image on the right is shifted a little to the left. It is this slight difference that makes the three-dimensional effect possible when seen through a viewer. Notice also the care taken in composition. The foreground trees form a perfect frame for the falls. Courtesy of the J. Paul Getty Museum, Los Angeles.

Watkins also made use of another innovation that became immensely popular during the mid-nineteenth century—stereoscopic photographs. These were actually two photographs, set side by side, that had been taken with a camera equipped with two lenses. The lenses were spaced 2 1/2" apart, about the distance between your eyes. In other words, the camera was made to imitate the way we see with two eyes, and it is this binocular vision that gives us such good depth perception. As you look out on the world, each eye is sending the brain a slightly different image (as you can see if you look at something first through one eye and then the other), but the brain fuses the two images into one. Seen through one eye, the world looks rather flat. Having two eyes increases our sense of three-dimensional depth, especially of distances between objects. Although photographs are flat, when a stereoscopic pair is viewed through a special viewer, the brain is fooled into thinking they are three dimensional. As with our natural vision, the two images are joined in the brain, creating a startling illusion for the viewer of being there, actually standing on the edge of a cliff or in the depths of a canyon.

Stereo scenes were so popular that most houses had a basket of stereo cards along with a viewer on a table in the parlor for guests to enjoy. Thousands of these cards were made during the nineteenth century. Like most photographers, Watkins made many more stereo views than any other kind of photograph. Although his large landscape prints made him famous, it was the stereo views that introduced most people to the natural beauty of the West.

Watkins photographed in the West for over fifty years, until the late 1890s. In addition to his own landscape work, he took on commissions for a number of government projects and private industries. For example, in 1863 he was hired to photograph along the California coast near Mendocino by lumber interests that wanted the area publicized. In 1867 the Oregon Steam Company, a railroad, took him along on an expedition up the Willamette and Columbia rivers to photograph the scenery and their railroad. This often conflicting mix of art and industry became common practice among western photographers, who needed to make a living like anyone else. Watkins took some of his finest landscapes along the Columbia River Gorge, and the Oregon Steam Company got its publicity for rail travel. Photography served a variety of masters.

Exhibits and books of western landscape photography tend to give a one-sided impression of the relationship between the photographers and the land in which they worked. What we usually see are pictures of natural beauty in which evidence of human occupation has been carefully avoided—or at least minimized. This often leads to the assumption that the photographers were on the side of conservationists who wanted to preserve the natural world as it was. But in fact, considerably more photographs were produced to promote economic development than to foster an appreciation of wilderness.

Today we live in an age of ecological awareness. The defenders of nature and the forces of industry have at each other in the daily news.

But in the nineteenth century most white Americans saw no conflict between love of nature and industrial development. The country was huge, almost empty, and the spread of western civilization was a good thing. Watkins's name, for example, was practically synonymous with the American vision of Eden in the wilderness, and yet at the same time his work for the railroads and lumber interests openly promoted development and tourism. There was no conflict here.

Most western photographers were businessmen and entrepreneurs who worked with an eye on the market, selling pictures of Indians and breathtaking mountain views to dealers in the East. And they worked on commission for railroads, mining and lumber companies, hotels, resorts, government agencies, and civic organizations. Often, mills and mines and railroad bridges were photographed in such a way that they seemed to blend in with the landscape, satisfying a desire for harmony. One historian writes of Watkins,

> Commonly, he photographed lumbering operations against a background of dense woods rather than in detached work yards. Thus the nineteenth-century apprehension that industry defiled nature in the process of learning nature's secrets was eased in a visual narrative of reconciliation.[7]

She also makes the point that Watkins brought the same sense of visual beauty to photographing industrial sites as he did to mountains and waterfalls. In both cases, the compositions convey a feeling of order, balance, and serenity.

By the end of the 1860s Watkins was doing well. He was making good money from the sale of his photographs and from his commercial assignments. He continued to travel widely, as far north as Montana and Victoria, British Columbia, and throughout the Southwest. Some of his travels were supported by his friend Collis Huntington, an executive with the Central Pacific Railroad. Huntington gave Watkins his own flatcar to carry his wagon loaded with photographic equipment from place to place. In this way, Watkins gained access to wilderness areas he would not have been able to reach otherwise, and the Central

Pacific got spectacular photographs with which it could entice prospective customers, giving them a taste of the splendors that awaited them as they rolled along in the luxurious comfort of their Pullman cars.

Watkins's travel eventually took its toll on him. The work was hard, taking him away from home for months at a time. In 1882 he wrote to his wife, "I have never had the time seem so long to me on any trip I ever made from home, and I am not half done with my work. . . . It drags along awful slow, between the smoke and the rain and the wind, and as if the elements were not enough to worry me, a spark from an engine set fire to my tent last week and burned it half up."[8] The tent he referred to was his darkroom.

In 1874 when the Bank of California failed, Watkins had fallen on hard times. He lost his Yosemite gallery—along with all of his negatives—to a couple of his competitors. He had to start over, but after that disaster he never had much financial success. At one point, he was reduced to living in a railroad boxcar. Bad luck dogged him until nearly the end of his life. Old and nearly blind, at the age of seventy-seven, he was working on the sale of his negatives to Stanford University when the earthquake and fire of 1906 struck San Francisco. Once again, he lost his life's work. He never recovered from this loss. Watkins spent his last years in the Napa State Hospital at Imola, California, until his death in 1916.

During his long life, Carleton Watkins made thousands of photographs and raised the art of photography to a high level. His pictures of Yosemite defined an American ideal of what paradise should look like. He was typical of most western photographers in his blending of art and commerce, and in the vision he presented to the world he gave white America what it wanted to see—a West that promised both natural wonders and civilized refinement. Fittingly, the first landmark in Yosemite to be named after a living person was named after him—Mount Watkins.

CHAPTER THREE

Imagining America

EVER SINCE CARLETON WATKINS turned Yosemite Valley into an American Eden, the celebration of unspoiled wilderness has been a continuing theme in American photography. But photographers weren't the first to make wild nature a subject for art and contemplation. Painters were. By the time photographers were carting their gear out to the mountains and valleys of the West, certain ideas about the land and its meaning had been worked out by painters in the East.

The first American images that depicted wilderness as a place you might like to go to were created by painters in the 1820s. Up until that time American painters had concentrated exclusively on portraits and historical figures and events—especially scenes and heros from the American Revolution. But as the East was settled, land cleared, towns and cities built, and the Indian either wiped out, exiled, or domesticated, painters turned to the natural world as a source of both spiritual renewal and national identity. As art critic Robert Hughes has written, "Americans saw in their wilderness the very prototype of Nature, the place where the designs of God survived in their virgin and unedited state."[1] The novelist James Fenimore Cooper (1789–1851) spoke of "the holy calm of nature." It was out of this romantic sensibility that the first American landscapes came, from the brushes of a group of New York painters known as the Hudson River School.

In 1818, a young man named Thomas Cole emigrated from England with his family and settled in Philadelphia. He was seventeen years old. He worked for a few years as an engraver, though what he wanted to be was a painter. He took advantage of what advice he could pick up here and there, and at the age of twenty-four took his paintings and drawings to New York City and found a dealer for them.

Cole became the first American landscape painter. He painted peaceful, welcoming scenes of natural beauty along the Hudson River and in the Catskill Mountains. In Cole's pictures the viewer is invited to contemplate nature, to regard it as a place for enjoyment and spiritual renewal. Cole was a painter of the settled East. Nature was largely tamed. His vision is of a harmonious, tranquil relation between man and nature.

In 1836 Cole did a series of paintings called *The Course of Empire*. It depicted in five stages the rise and fall of civilizations. The first painting is called *The Savage State*. The land is raw and there are no permanent settlements. The second painting is titled *The Arcadian or Pastoral State*. Arcadia was a region of ancient Greece where it was thought people lived peaceful and happy lives in harmony with nature. It had been idealized in art and literature in England since the sixteenth century. Cole's painting shows a country scene, bathed by the rich light of dawn or sunset, with a harbor and mountains in the background. In the distance a shepherd grazes his flock, a young girl plays a flute while others dance, and a man sits contemplating the scene. This is the dream of an ideal life, civilized yet in harmony with nature. After this it's all downhill to the last and fifth painting, *Desolation*.

For Cole and others like him, America was virgin territory. Unlike Europe, the American landscape wasn't cluttered with the crumbling ruins and moldy medieval castles of dead civilizations. It was fresh and new, the emblem of the divine promise of a new world. Thomas Cole was the first to give artistic expression to this vision.

The idea that nature is the source of spiritual life took strong root in America in the nineteenth century. It found its way into poems, novels, essays, paintings, and photographs. This belief was one of the cen-

The Falls of Kaaterskill (1826) by Thomas Cole. Cole painted this scene after a summer spent walking and sketching in the Hudson Valley and the Catskill Mountains. It was one of the first works in what later became known as the Hudson River School of painting. Courtesy of the Warner Collection of Gulf States Paper Corporation, Tuscaloosa, Alabama.

tral tenets of the Romantic movement that swept across Europe and
the United States in the early- to mid-nineteenth century. This was a
complex movement in the arts, literature, and philosophy that generally favored, among other things, feeling over reason, nature and the
individual over society, and the primitive over the civilized. In the
United States these ideas found their strongest expression in the works
of writers like Henry David Thoreau, Ralph Waldo Emerson, and
William Cullen Bryant. Listen, for example, to this excerpt from
William Cullen Bryant's "Forest Hymn" of 1825:

> Father, thy hand
> Hath reared these venerable columns, thou
> Didst weave this verdant roof. Thou didst look down
> Upon the naked earth, and, forthwith, rose
> All these fair ranks of trees. They, in thy sun,
> Budded, and shook their green leaves in thy breeze
> And shot toward heaven. The century-living crow
> Whose birth was in their tops, grew old and died
> Among their branches, till, at last, they stood,
> As now they stand, massy, and tall, and dark,
> Fit shrine for humble worshiper to hold
> Communion with his Maker.[2]

God is to be found in the cathedral of the forest.

The glories of the American landscape were celebrated in many
other places, one of which was a popular book published in 1852. The
book bore the cumbersome title, *The home book of the picturesque: or,
American scenery, art, and literature. Comprising a series of essays by
Washington Irving, W.C. Bryant, Fenimore Cooper . . . etc., with thirteen engravings on steel, from pictures by eminent artists.* The dedica-
tion to this book states that it is "Intended as an initiatory suggestion
for popularizing some of the characteristics of American Landscape
and American Art." It was much more than a picture book. It had a
point to make: The essays and illustrations declared the American land-

scape to be a source of religious, moral, and patriotic inspiration. The paintings, which were reproduced as engravings in the book, were by artists associated with the East, such as Thomas Cole, Asher Durand, and Frederick Church. But the basic values put forward by the book—religion, morality, patriotism—entered into the complex mix of ideas and dreams and motives that shaped the image of the West.

As America expanded westward, artists encountered nature on a scale not seen in the East. Everything was bigger. Like photographers who built mammoth cameras, there were painters who tried to meet the challenge of the land with giant canvases. The most famous of these western painters was the son of a German immigrant family named Albert Bierstadt (1830-1902). Bierstadt grew up in New Bedford, Massachusetts, but as a young man he traveled to Germany and then to Italy to study painting. When he returned, he realized that the western landscape was unique to America and that no one was painting it. In 1858 he joined Col. Frederick Lander's surveying expedition to the Rocky Mountains and made hundreds of sketches and watercolor studies along the way.

Back in New York, Bierstadt developed his sketches into huge oil paintings, measuring over 6' x 10'. These paintings of soaring, snow-capped peaks and fertile valleys captured the imagination of the public. This was wild nature, all right, but it was far from the fearsome Great American Desert of legend. This was magnificent country, ripe for settlement and just waiting for those who would venture into it. In one of his most famous works, *Crossing the Plains* (1867), a wagon train labors toward a spectacular sunset that sets the sky afire. Golden light floods the land and the sky is aflame with clouds tinted yellow, red, and violet. The wagon train rolls on into the sunset, America's future. It's as close to an image of a journey to the promised land as any American painting ever made.

Many of these spectacular paintings by Bierstadt and others who followed were more than magnificent scenery. They supported an idea, widespread at the time, that it was the destiny of white Americans to extend their civilization to the edge of the continent.

Government policy toward the West underwent a great change during the nineteenth century. In the early years of the Republic the main concern was that the population (then about six million) would become scattered too thinly over the country if large numbers of people moved west. When the treaty to purchase the Louisiana Territory from France was presented to Congress in 1803, the debate was intense. Louisiana Territory stretched from the Mississippi River to the Rocky Mountains, and from the Gulf of Mexico to the Canadian border. At a single stroke, the purchase would double the size of the country. Many people in public life feared that spreading the population over such a large area would weaken the country. They believed a nation's strength lay in the concentration of its people, not in its physical size.

Another fear aroused by the Louisiana Purchase was that it would in time shift the balance of power away from the existing states. Senator Uriah Tracy of Connecticut warned that "the relative strength which this admission gives to a Southern and Western interest, is contradictory to the principles of our original Union."[3]

In response to these fears, President Thomas Jefferson proposed a constitutional amendment blocking the westward movement of the population. One provision of this amendment was that "the rights of occupancy in the soil and of self-government are confirmed to the Indian inhabitants as they now exist." Furthermore, Jefferson added, the "great object" was "to prevent emigrations, excepting to a certain portion of the ceded territory."[4]

In spite of these misgivings, the nation continued to expand and people flowed into the new territories. The huge expanse of the Southwest, from Texas to California, was added in 1848 following the defeat of Mexico in the Mexican War. And in 1853, the area of the contiguous forty-eight states was completed by the Gadsden Purchase: The U.S. bought from Mexico land in southern New Mexico and Arizona that was favored as a route by backers of a southern transcontinental railroad.

Uncertainty and disagreement over national boundaries and purpose continued well past the close of the eighteenth century. Should the U.S. remain within its comfortable eighteenth century boundaries, or keep going until there was nowhere else to go? Those who favored expansion finally won out. If the country needed a reason to keep going, it was given in 1845 by a newspaper editor named John O'Sullivan, writing in a magazine titled *United States Magazine and Democratic Review*. O'Sullivan declared that it was "our manifest destiny to overspread the continent allotted by Providence for the free development of our yearly multiplying millions."

O'Sullivan was writing to support the annexation of Texas, which at the time was Mexican territory. But "manifest destiny" quickly became a catch-phrase to justify any act of expansion. It was used to justify the Mexican War, the slaughter and removal of the American Indian, the later annexation of Puerto Rico, the Philippine Islands, and Hawaii, and the building of the Panama Canal. The cluster of ideas that gathered under the rubric of manifest destiny were these: that Americans of northern European descent are superior; that North America is a "promised land" given by God to these, his "chosen people"; and that it is the duty of those "chosen people" to spread Christianity and their civilization far and wide across the continent. Many painters and photographers in the nineteenth century embodied in their work the idea that the westward movement of white civilization was a triumphant advance overseen by an approving God. They saw no conflict between a love of nature and a pair of train tracks running out to the horizon.

Photography in the West drew on these many sources. Before the camera came on the scene, an American landscape art had been established by the Hudson River painters, and a complex cluster of attitudes about the land, the nation, and the West was firmly in place. These attitudes influenced the way photographers viewed and depicted the landscape, and they influenced the way people looked at photographs. A landscape says as much about the person who made it as it does about the subject; it discloses and promulgates a certain way of thinking and feeling about the land.

CHAPTER FOUR

War Photographers and Western Journeys

THE CIVIL WAR ended in April 1865, and the attention of the nation turned from the war to the West. Even before the guns had stopped firing, crews were busy laying tracks through Kansas and Nebraska, stretching out across the Plains. The advance of the railroad drew more emigrants, and the U.S. government began to take measures to strengthen its control over the western territories. The growing number of settlers threatened the way of life of the Plains Indians, some of whom fought against this invasion of their homelands. Even though the Removal Act of 1830 had promised the Indians sanctuary west of the Mississippi, the attitude of the U.S. government toward expansion had changed. Now the Indians were in the way, and the army was sent out to take care of the problem.

The construction of the railroads created a great deal of interest among easterners, first in the country around Kansas and Nebraska, then further west. They wanted to see what the land and the people looked like, and the railroads provided the way to get there in relative comfort. Railroad promoters hired photographers to record the construction and produce pictures for publicity. What the government and the railroad men wanted from these photographers were pictures that would encourage settlement, development, and tourism. The railroad was truly the engine of empire, making the West accessible and linking communities all across the country. The final spike completing the transcontinental railroad was driven at Promontory Point, Utah, in 1869. This was as big a step for the nineteenth century as astronaut Neil Armstrong's giant step on the moon a hundred years later would be for the twentieth.

And so photographers went to work along the routes of the railroads. One, Alexander Gardner, produced a photo titled with the popular phrase, "Westward the Course of Empire Takes Its Way," that says it all. A locomotive steaming across the Plains or through the mountains became an image of national pride. Photographs of construction along the rail lines often bore captions pointing to "the advance of civilization." These photographs helped to calm fears of "The Great American Desert" and encourage people to move and travel west, which of course was good for the railroad business and other enterprises that grew up along the rail lines.

Alexander Gardner was a veteran Civil War photographer who was hired by the Union Pacific Railroad in 1867 to work along the line in Kansas. His work involved much more than just pictures of trains and bridges and stations. Gardner photographed the countryside and in every town along the tracks. He traveled from town to town in a wagon, which served as his darkroom. He made stereoscopic views and large prints from 8"x 10" and 11"x 14" wet-plate negatives. While some photographers worked independently in hopes of selling prints, much of the best work was done for railroad commissions. Along with photographers like A. J. Russell, A. A. Hart, and F. Jay Haynes, Gardner pro-

---

Following page: *Westward the Course of Empire Takes Its Way* (1867, albumen, 32.9 x 47.5 cm) by Alexander Gardner. Out on the prairie, workers are laying track for the Union Pacific Railroad. The title is from a poem by the Irish philosopher George Berkeley. Gardner probably took it from the title of the mural by Emanuel Leutz in the U.S. Capitol. Several other artists used the same title for works depicting the railroad heading west, extending the American empire to the Pacific. Courtesy of the J. Paul Getty Museum, Los Angeles.

duced a rich record of the building of the railroads and life on the Plains in the years following the war.

~

THE BEST OF THESE men had gotten their experience by working as war photographers. The war had been a tough school where photographers had to work under the most difficult and dangerous conditions. In spite of the hardships and risks, they had produced thousands of photographs–the greatest photographic record of war ever made up to that time. This work was the result of one man's mission. His name was Mathew Brady.

Before the war, Mathew Brady had been a successful portrait photographer. He opened his first gallery in New York in 1844. He worked hard and conducted endless experiments to improve his technique. He won many prizes for his work in public exhibitions.

In 1845 Brady came up with the idea of building a collection of portraits of famous people and he was extremely successful at this. For example, he photographed every American president who held office during the nineteenth century, except for William Henry Harrison who died just one month after his inauguration. (Some of the earlier presidents were photographed after they had left office.) Brady was so devoted to this project that he opened another gallery in Washington, D.C., just to be close to the politicians and statesmen he wanted to photograph.

When war broke out in April 1861, Brady had already shown a great interest in recording the history of his times. It was natural that he should undertake the project of photographing the war. He once said, "I felt that I had to go. A spirit in my feet said 'go,' and I went." Brady became the first photojournalist, the first to use photography to document news.

As the war expanded, Brady realized that he couldn't do it all himself, so he hired a small army of assistants to help him. These men underwent rigorous on-the-job training as field photographers under incredibly harsh conditions. Wet-plate photography required them to unpack the mules, set up the dark tent, flow the collodion on the glass negative, load it in the camera, take the picture, duck back into the dark tent, develop the plate. Much of this is delicate work that requires a steady hand, and it often had to be done with a battle raging nearby–guns firing, shells bursting, men shouting and screaming.

At the time of the Civil War, it wasn't possible to photograph actual action scenes of battles because of the time needed to expose the plates. People moving quickly wouldn't be recorded, and during the height of battle people move quickly. So most of the photographs we have of battles are fairly static. There are also many pictures of soldiers in camp, of the aftermath of battles, and of the devastation of war.

Even though they weren't often in the thick of the fighting the way combat photographers were in later wars, the Civil War photographers faced plenty of danger and hardship. They were often close enough to the action to be hit by shell fragments or stray bullets. And since their dark tents were usually mounted on horse-drawn wagons, disasters happened frequently when the horses were spooked by a shell blast and took off in fright while the photographer was inside trying to prepare his plates.

So when the war ended, there was a corps of battle-hardened photographers with four years' experience, looking for work. And work was waiting for them.

∿

IN 1867, two years after the end of the war, Congress passed a bill that authorized expeditions to further explore the West. Their purpose would be a little different from the exploration that took place before the war. The central aim of the expeditions during the 1850s had been to map the country and to find routes for roads and railways. The post-war expeditions, called the U.S. Geological Surveys, continued mapping but were also charged with studying the geology, natural resources, and native inhabitants of the West. There were four of them, named for their leaders: Clarence King, Ferdinand Hayden, John Wesley Powell, and Lt. George Wheeler. Each one was assigned to a different area of the country. They worked each summer from 1867 to 1879, when Congress disbanded this set of surveys and established a new administration and a new U.S. Geological Survey.

The main reason for the shift from mapping to scientific exploration was the need of rapidly growing industry in the United States for raw materials. Factories and mills were running full speed ahead, and the undeveloped land west of the Mississippi held promise of great mineral wealth lying beneath the soil. To develop these resources, settlers would need to be attracted to the West, and so a second purpose of the geological surveys was to provide publicity. The role of artists and photographers in the surveys became more than simply documenting the land; now their work was used to make the West look attractive to easterners.

The first geological survey was the exploration of the fortieth parallel under the command of Clarence King of the Army Corps of Engineers. The fortieth parallel is the latitude that runs right through the middle of the United States, from northern California through Nevada and Utah and Colorado, and along the Kansas-Nebraska border. It would be the route of the first transcontinental railroad.

The photographer on this expedition was Timothy O'Sullivan. Not much is known of O'Sullivan's early life until he became an apprentice to Mathew Brady in about 1855 at the age of fifteen, and went on to photograph the war as one of Brady's crew for a couple of years. However, O'Sullivan and some of the other photographers became dissatisfied because Brady insisted on having his own name on all photographs taken by his employees. This meant that they would get no credit for their work. So O'Sullivan and Alexander Gardner split from Brady's outfit to form their own. After the war, Gardner published a book of a hundred photographs called *Gardner's Photographic Sketch Book of the War*. These were among the best photographs ever made of the war, and over half of them were Timothy O'Sullivan's.

Temporary and Permanent Bridges and Citadel Rock, Green River, Wyoming (1867/68) by A.J. Russell. Citadel Rock and the locomotive sit comfortably side by side, reflecting the view of most white Americans–no conflict between nature and progress. Courtesy of the Yale Collection of Western Americana, Beinecke Rare Book and Manuscript Library.

The first geological survey, with O'Sullivan along, set out from California in 1867. The expedition traveled first through northern California and Nevada, stopping for a short time in Nevada City, which had attracted flocks of miners seeking riches in gold and silver. The famous Comstock Lode had already produced ninety million dollars worth of gold. O'Sullivan took advantage of the stopover to take the first photographs ever done inside a mine, several hundred feet below the surface. To do this he used a magnesium flare, which was especially dangerous in a mine where inflammable gas could cause an explosion.

From Nevada City the party headed east toward the Rocky Mountains. This was rugged country, especially for O'Sullivan with all his photographic equipment. To help with his load, he had been assigned two mules and a packer. Luckily, we have an account of O'Sullivan's trials and adventures on this expedition. In September 1869, *Harper's New Monthly Magazine* published an article called "Photographs from the High Rockies." The writer, John Samson, described the journey and included thirteen woodblock engravings copied from O'Sullivan's photographs. One of the incidents described in the article occurred on a boat trip O'Sullivan took with several other members of the party down the Truckee River to photograph Pyramid Lake, Nevada. At one point the boat, named the *Nettie*, was wedged between two rocks and the oars were swept away. O'Sullivan jumped into the water. Here is Samson's version of events:

> Our photographic friend, being a swimmer of no ordinary power, suc-
> ceeded in reaching the shore, not opposite the *Nettie*, though it was but
> forty yards from the shore, for he was carried a hundred yards down the
> rapids. A rope was thrown to him from the boat, and thus he rescued the
> little craft with her crew from their perilous situation. The sharp rocks
> had torn the little clothing of which he had not divested himself, and had
> so cut and bruised his body that he was glad to crawl into the brier tan-
> gle that fringed the river's brink. When at last he gained the point near-
> est to the boat his excited friends threw shoreward his pocket-book,
> freighted with three hundred dollars in twenty dollar gold pieces. "That

was rough," said he; "for I never found that 'dust' again, though I prospected a long time, barefooted, for it."[1]

The party continued its journey, and O'Sullivan took some fine pictures at Pyramid Lake.

The expedition struggled through the Rocky Mountains, often traveling by night so that the colder temperature would have frozen a crust on the snow hard enough to support men and animals. Even so, in places the crust was still too thin and they were often bogged down, sometimes disappearing into drifts thirty or forty feet deep. Crossing one divide, they covered only two and a half miles in thirteen hours. What's more, the thin air at 10,000 or 11,000 feet slowed them down and caused many of the party to come down with altitude sickness.

In spite of all this, O'Sullivan made first-rate photographs of the wild mountain landscape. In the *Harper's Magazine* article, he spoke about photographing in the Humboldt and Carson Sinks, areas where there had been volcanic activity.

> It was a pretty location to work in, and viewing there was as pleasant work as could be desired; the only drawback was an unlimited number of the most voracious and particularly poisonous mosquitoes that we met with during our entire trip. Add to this the entire impossibility to save one's precious body from frequent attacks of that most enervating of all fevers, know as the "mountain ail," and you will see why we did not work up more of that country. We were, in fact, driven out by the mosquitoes and fever. Which of the two should be considered as the most unbearable it is impossible to state.[2]

O'Sullivan stayed with the expedition through 1869 and made hundreds of photographs. Pictures of the western landscape (called "views") were very popular in the East, and people eagerly collected them, mainly in the form of stereoscopic prints. The shadowy West had become real. Paintings and drawings could be manipulated; the artist could change the scene to make it look more interesting, more dramatic. But photographs told the truth. In these views, Americans felt they could see the West for themselves.

After the survey of the fortieth parallel, O'Sullivan went south. A long way south. He traveled to Panama with an expedition whose mission was to make a survey for one of the great engineering projects of the nineteenth century–the Panama Canal. He worked for a year with this survey, then returned to the U.S. and in 1873 joined Lt. George Wheeler, who was leading another series of surveys in the Southwest. In New Mexico, O'Sullivan made some of his most famous pictures, photographs of the Pueblo Indian ruins at Canyon de Chelly.

He also accompanied Wheeler on yet another hair-raising adventure, a journey by boat *up* the Colorado River. The party met with rougher going than they had expected–heavy rapids and waterfalls. It took thirty-one days to travel 260 miles. Wheeler lost all of his papers when his boat capsized. Toward the end of the journey, at a place they named "Starvation Camp," their rations were so low that Wheeler had to guard them himself. He wrote in his diary that there was hardly enough to make a decent pillow. On this trip O'Sullivan took some of the earliest photographs of the Grand Canyon. One of his best was of the river and the canyon beyond with his boat, named *Picture*, in the foreground.

O'Sullivan brought a lot more than a rugged character and technical skill to his work. He had a fine sense of locating the best view of his subject and creating strong compositions in the viewfinder of his camera. O'Sullivan did most of his work in the remote desert of the Southwest and the rocky wilderness of Nevada, Utah, Colorado and Idaho. This is not country that suggests an escape to Eden to contemplate nature; it is harsh and unforgiving. Yet O'Sullivan's pictures give a sense of the beauty and power to be found in a land stripped down to its basic forms. His work lacks the softness and grace of Watkins's Yosemite views, but his direct, straightforward approach perfectly suited the character of the country in which he worked. He chose with great care the point of view and lighting that would best reveal the form of his subject, without romanticizing or overly dramatizing it. Every detail is visible. O'Sullivan's West is dominated by the bold forms of

Ancient Ruins in the Cañon de Chelle, New Mexico (1873) by Timothy O'Sullivan. These Indian cliff dwellings, now part of the Navajo reservation, were built between A.D. 350 and 1300. Courtesy of George Eastman House.

craggy rocks, barren ridges, and steep impassable canyons. His best pictures are composed of strong, integrated forms that convey a sense of an underlying order in nature.

For all that he accomplished, it's hard to believe that Timothy O'Sullivan lived only forty-two years. He died of tuberculosis in 1882 shortly after being appointed official photographer for the U.S. Treasury Department.

CHAPTER FIVE

Photographers of the Local Scene

THE PHOTOGRAPHERS who went west with the exploratory expeditions provided the excitement. They were the stars. The best of them had their work published in prestigious magazines like *Harper's Weekly* and *Scribner's*, and shown in elegant galleries and museums. Like travelers who return from faraway places bearing tales of wonder and adventure, they fed the public's hunger for pictures of the unknown and the exotic.

But wilderness adventure wasn't the only side of life in the Wild West. From the 1830s on, a sprinkling of white settlers lived and farmed along the river valleys in eastern Kansas and Nebraska. But once the Civil War was over and the transcontinental railroad was built, towns and villages spread across the Great Plains. The Homestead Act of 1862 granted 160 acres of land to anyone who would live on it and improve it for five years. Publicity generated by the railroads and the government lured the hopeful west to the newly designated "garden" just waiting for them to break the sod and plant their crops. With the emancipation of the slaves and the end of the Civil War, the westward migration also included black Americans, many of them lured by promises of all-black towns.

The wagons came, and it wasn't long after a few rickety buildings rose to mark the beginning of a new town that a man with a camera was sure to appear on the scene.

First came the wandering daguerreotypists who went from town to town like traveling merchants and circuit preachers. Hauling their equipment in horse-drawn wagons, or sometimes even in hand carts, they would set up temporary studios, usually tents, for as long as people came to have their pictures taken—then move on. But as towns grew larger, photographers moved in and built permanent studios. Nevertheless, for many of them it was still an itinerant existence, especially in the small towns. A common pattern went like this: A photographer would move into a town and build or buy a studio. Notices would appear in the local paper. Curiosity would bring in clients for awhile, but soon the novelty would fade and the photographer would find himself without enough business to support his studio. Often photographers would try to supplement their incomes by working for a large company, like a railroad or mining operation, or for the government. They would also photograph local Indians and cowboys and local landmarks and try to sell prints on the open market. But it often happened that after four or five years the photographer would be forced to pack up and move to another town, selling his business to a fresh hopeful who would begin the cycle all over again.

The photographers who did manage to establish themselves permanently, usually in the larger cities, became part of the community, like any other business people—raising families, joining churches and civic organizations, serving on boards and holding office. Being part of local society, they were in a position to record an intimate view of everyday life as it was lived by ordinary people. They photographed street scenes, landscapes, people at work and play, special occasions and public events. Their pictures give an up-close-and-personal view of how people lived and worked, how they dressed, and how they celebrated.

The main business of these studios was portrait work. From the beginning, portraits were the photographer's bread and butter. In the early days having your picture taken was an expensive proposition, and only people with plenty of money could afford it. However, this changed over time as equipment and processes became better and cheaper, and by the 1860s family portraits graced the mantles in practically all American homes.

During the Civil War a cheaper version of the daguerreotype, called a *tintype*, became all the rage among ordinary people. Everyone whose son was sent off to war wanted a picture to remember him by. Tintype photographers followed the army from camp to camp, taking "sun pictures" for soldiers to send back to mom and dad. So many photographs were mailed back and forth that it created a problem for the postal service, which announced that "not infrequently a number of bags go out from the Washington office entirely filled with sun pictures, enclosed in light but bulky cases."

At the same time, a fad for a kind of portrait called a *carte de visite* took the country by storm. *Carte de visite* is French for "visiting card." It was the custom for visitors to a home to present their hosts with cards bearing their names. These cards were usually collected in a basket near the door. The *carte de visite* photograph was a small picture pasted onto the card, so the visitor would leave not just a name, but a likeness as well. The *carte de visite* originated in France, patented by a man named Adolphe-Eugene Disderi, and the French term stuck. What Disderi developed was a way of taking a number of small photographs, usually eight to twelve, on the same plate. To do this he used a camera with several lenses and a mechanism for moving the plate from one position to another.

People began using these little portraits in place of visiting cards, so gradually the baskets by the door filled up with pictures. Then came the dilemma: What to do with all these pictures? Someone had the bright idea of putting them all in a book, and so the family photo album was born. This became a treasured possession, even in very poor homes. Here, for example, is what one Montana pioneer wrote:

> Our cabin measured 16 x 20 feet in the clear. The logs were chinked and painted with clay. The floor was of earth, beaten hard and smooth,—a box cupboard held our stock of dishes and cooking utensils. Beside it stood the churn. The flour barrel was converted into a center-table

whereon reposed the family Bible and photograph album with their white lace covers.[1]

For settlers in the West the album had a special value, for it contained the likenesses of all those they had left behind—parents and grandparents, aunts and uncles, cousins, nephews, nieces, neighbors and friends. It was their link to the past.

In addition to portraits, town photographers might be called upon for a variety of jobs. William Henry Jackson, who opened his first studio in Omaha, Nebraska, in 1867, described the day-to-day operation of a town photographer:

> Straight portrait jobs; group pictures of lodges, church societies, and political clubs; and outdoor shots that gratified civic pride. There were many commissions to photograph shop fronts and, occasionally, interiors. Now and then, too, somebody would order pictures of his new house; or of his big barn, and along with it the livestock.[2]

Jackson also took frequent trips to photograph the local Indians and sold prints through his gallery and eastern dealers.

Almost every western town today has a historical society or library with a collection of such pictures by local photographers. The names of many of them have been lost, their work forgotten for years until someone snooping in a dusty corner of an attic or workshop would come across a box of prints or a stack of glass negatives. "Anonymous" is probably the most common name among western photographers of the local scene. But there are also those whose names have endured, some of them exceptionally talented. In their work they captured the essential spirit of a certain time and place.

One such photographer was Laton Alton Huffman.

Picture a lone rider crossing a wide expanse of prairie, his horse festooned with a fifty-pound camera and bottles of chemicals and a dark tent. He's headed out to a ranch or a roundup, a buffalo hunt or an Indian encampment. Such a picture, if it existed, would tell us something of what lay at the heart of this man's life and work.

View of Harrison Street, Leadville, Colorado (1879) by George D. Wakely. This street scene is typical of the work of local photographers throughout the West. Some of the figures in the foreground registered as ghost images, indicating that they moved during the long exposure needed to take the picture. Courtesy of Denver Public Library, Western History Collection, X-471.

Huffman spent most of his adult life in eastern Montana—Miles City and Billings—and became a part of that state's history, not only as a photographer but also as a school board member, county commissioner and state legislator. The editor of the newspaper, the *Miles City Star*, said that Huffman "was more than an ordinary character—*he was an institution.*"[3]

As closely as he is associated with Montana, Huffman was not a native. Like most white westerners at that time he was from somewhere else. He was born in Iowa and as a boy he first learned photography from his father. Later, he served an apprenticeship in a studio in

Moorhead, Minnesota, but he was a restless young man, always facing west, fascinated by stories of the open country beyond the horizon.

In 1878, at the age of twenty-eight, Huffman applied for a job as photographer at Fort Keogh, an army post in eastern Montana Territory. It wasn't much of a job. It paid nothing. The only benefit was the right to set up shop in a ramshackle log shack that had been abandoned by the previous post photographer, who had gone broke. And Huffman could keep the profits from his work—if there were any. The job was hardly a prize, but at least it gave him a base of operations from which to begin.

Huffman loved the open country of Montana. As soon as he could, he bought a horse and camping outfit and rode north across the vast prairie between the Yellowstone and Missouri rivers until he came across a camp of buffalo hunters. His pictures of these hunters marked the beginning of his life's work.

After a couple of years at Fort Keogh, Huffman opened his first studio in Miles City. Business was slow, so he hunted buffalo for meat and hides and worked sporadically as a guide. He tried ranching but gave it up after a few years. Through it all he kept photographing and gradually found a market for his work.

Huffman opened several studios at various times in Miles City and Billings, but his real passion remained life on the range. He was there with his camera during the last two decades of the open range, before the grid of barbed wire fell across the boundless country. "This Yellowstone-Bighorn country was then unpenned of wire, and unspoiled by railway, dam or ditch," he wrote. He photographed the landscape—the "Big Open," as he called it—and the daily life of cowboys and ranchers and sheepherders who lived there. And he was there, he remembered, as "the army of buffalo hunters—red men and white—were waging the final war of extermination upon the last great herds of American bison seen upon this continent."[4]

Once the buffalo were gone, cattlemen and sheepherders drove their livestock in large numbers into Montana Territory. They pushed the herds hundreds of miles, from as far east as Iowa and as far south as southern Texas, onto the grassy plains of eastern Montana. For twenty years—after the extermination of the buffalo and before barbed wire—ranching flourished on the open range. This is where Huffman achieved his finest work, in a body of photographs that constitute a complete portrait of the many facets of ranch life: pictures of owners, trail bosses, cowboys, roundups, cattle drives, and branding. He accomplished the difficult task of taking action pictures of cowboys cutting steers and breaking broncos.

Huffman not only photographed; he also wrote detailed descriptions of what was going on in the pictures. For example, he wrote this about *Saddling the Wild Horse, 1894:*

> There are many ways of accomplishing this feat. The cowboy in this picture, a professional broncho-buster, proceeded to rope, blindfold and bridle the gray horse, then took him outside the corral at my request, and flung on the saddle, holding the horse by the bridle and hackamore [a bridle without a bit]. The picture was made just at the instant when he gave the first pull at the Latino, cinching the saddle.[5]

Huffman's work, like that of many other photographers in the West, provided easterners with some understanding of western skills and trades. It also preserved for future generations a glimpse of a short-lived way of life—ranching on the open range.

Given the equipment Huffman had to work with, capturing action pictures was no easy task. There had been some advances in photography: By the 1880s the old wet-plate process had been replaced by manufactured dry plates that didn't have to be developed on the spot, freeing the photographer from having to lug a darkroom outfit along. These faster dry plates made hand-held action photography possible, but they were still slow by modern standards. Getting a good shot of a man roping a wild horse was still a matter of considerable skill, timing, and luck.

Huffman wrote very little about the technical aspects or difficulties of early photography. He was more interested in the subjects of his pictures. But in a letter to his father dated June 7, 1885, there is a note of

Saddling the Wild Horse (1894) by L.A. Huffman. Courtesy of the Montana Historical Society, Helena.

excitement in his description of the results obtained with his new equipment:

> I just returned a few days ago from a 12 days ride with the Powder River roundup—I shall soon show you what can be done from the saddle without ground glass and tripod—Please notice when you get the specimens that they were made with the lens wide open and many of the best exposed when my horse was in motion."[6]

This letter reveals a great deal about the skill and ingenuity of the photographer. For one thing, it tells us that he was able to hand-hold a heavy camera designed to be supported on a tripod and get good pictures from a moving horse. What's more, he shot blind, without looking at the scene through the viewfinder: The ground glass, on which the image would appear, had been removed.

With the coming of barbed wire, irrigation, and land development in the 1890s, the days of the open frontier came to an end. Huffman closed his studio in Miles City in about 1905 and concentrated on printing and selling his earlier photographs. Although he lived until 1931, he did little new work.

Huffman was of a divided mind about the development of Montana Territory. On the one hand, as a member of the Montana House of Representatives he introduced a bill promoting irrigation, which he knew would lead to more farming and the enclosure of the land. On the other hand, he regretted the loss of open spaces. In an article for the *Yellowstone Journal* he expressed his ambivalence: "I would that there were yet a few waste places left untouched by the settler and his cursed wire fence, good in its way, but not for me."[7] Elsewhere he remarked that the West "was a dream and a forgetting, a chapter forever closed."[8]

Huffman's work represents another phase of western photography, different from celebrations of magnificent landscapes or the forward thrust of the American empire. There is a sense of loss; L. A. Huffman is showing us the end of something rather than the beginning. He was, said one friend, "a modest man, rather mild spoken, kindly with gentlemanly manners, and not a trace of swagger." What he *did* say is fittingly plain and understated: "With crude home-made cameras, from saddle and in log shack," he wrote, "I saved something."[9]

~

PERHAPS THE MOST ambitious project to photograph a local scene was undertaken by a Nebraska photographer named Solomon D. Butcher. At the time the idea came to him, Butcher was broke and desperate. It was 1886, the year of the great drought on the Plains, when lack of rainfall dried up the fields and the hopes of more than a few homesteading farmers.

The town of Walworth, Nebraska, where Butcher had recently built a new photographic gallery, fell victim to the drought. It vanished overnight—literally vanished. Wood was scarce on the treeless prairie, so when a town died, which was not a rare occurrence, people dismantled their houses and shops and carted them by wagon to a new location. Butcher and his partner, A.W. Darling, had to sell their gallery, and the new owner moved it to another town.

Thirty years old, married with two small children, Butcher was suddenly left with nothing but a piece of land he had once unsuccessfully tried to farm. He knew he was not cut out for the homesteading life. In March 1880, when his father had given up a secure job with the railroad to take up a homestead "out west," Butcher had gone along. Butcher and his father, his brother, and brother-in-law set out in two covered wagons for the 700-mile journey to Nebraska. It took them seven weeks.

When they reached Nebraska, the men took claims in northeastern Custer County. After filing for their land, the first order of business was to construct some kind of temporary shelter—which turned out to be a wagon cover over a hole in the ground—while they built their first house on Solomon's father's claim.

Houses out on the prairie were built of sod—three-inch-thick blocks of grass and roots sliced from the ground in eighteen-inch-wide strips which were then cut into three-foot lengths. The blocks of sod were laid like bricks to form walls. The local people called this sod "Nebraska marble" and the houses "soddies."

It didn't take long for Butcher to realize that this life was not for him. He later wrote about these experiences: "I soon came to the conclusion that any man that would leave the luxuries of a boarding house, where they had hash every day, and a salary of $125 a month, to lay Nebraska sod for 75 cent a day, even if there was a 'gintleman' on top of the wall to do the work, was a fool."[10] He couldn't see spending five years working his claim, as required by the Homestead Act, so he returned the land to the government and left Nebraska to attend medical college in Minneapolis. However, something about the West still pulled at Butcher. As he later wrote, "I had seen enough of the wild west to unfit me for living contentedly in the East."[11] With his new wife, he headed back to Nebraska where the couple lived with his father and Solomon tried his hand at teaching school.

By the winter of 1882, Butcher was able to save and borrow enough money to buy a piece of land and build a crude photography gallery. He had learned the rudiments of photography after his graduation from high school, when for a short time he had been apprenticed to a tin-typist in Burton, Virginia, where he had grown up. The business was a struggle at first; Butcher had to supplement his income by farming for his father at the rate of fifty to seventy-five cents a day. But two years and two children later, he built his family a sod house in the town of Walworth, and with his partner built a wood-frame studio. It was shortly after this that the drought struck and Walworth disappeared, providing the pressure that resulted in Butcher's big idea. The plan Solomon Butcher conjured out of his desperation was to produce a comprehensive photographic history of Custer County, Nebraska. Later, he remembered this moment:

> From the time I thought of the plan, for seven days and seven nights it drove the sleep from my eyes. I laid out plans and covered sheet after sheet of paper, only to tear them up and consign them to the waste basket. At last, Eureka! Eureka! I had found it. I was so elated that I had lost all desire for rest and had to take morphine to make me sleep.[12]

Butcher had the inspiration but lacked the means to realize it. He went to his father, who had done well farming, and asked for a horse and wagon to carry his equipment out to the homesteads to photograph. His father was skeptical at first, but when Solomon was able to line up seventy-five of the area's farmers for his project in only two weeks, the elder Butcher agreed to help. In June 1886, Butcher took the first of 1,500 negatives that would comprise his *Pioneer History of Custer County, Nebraska*, published in 1901. In addition to photo-

Custer County, Nebraska (1888) by Solomon Butcher. As in almost all of Butcher's "sod house" photographs, family members are posed in front of the house in their best clothes, their possessions–horses, cattle, a wagon–assembled around them. Here the sod house is directly behind the people, and further are the barns. The blurred horse's head is due to movement during the long exposure. Courtesy of the Nebraska State Historical Society Photographic Collections.

graphs, Butcher's *History* also includes biographies and stories from his subjects. It is a rare historical record of a slice of life—pioneer settlement on the prairie—that lasted only a few years in the story of America's expansion.

Butcher was not a great artistic photographer. His pictures are straightforward and simply composed—in most cases, a family group standing or sitting in front of a sod house, often with their possessions arranged around them. What Butcher accomplished with this unadorned style was something more than individual portraits or awe-inspiring landscapes could do: He captured the fine details of a particular way of life, a personal history of people working in difficult country to realize their vision of the American Dream—a home, humble as it might be, a piece of land, a family.

To these people, having their pictures taken was a serious occasion. This was before the age of the casual snapshot, when photography was still the occupation of professionals and dedicated amateurs. In his autobiography *Time Exposure*, published in 1940, the photographer William Henry Jackson reminisced about portrait work during the early days:

> In this present day of magnificent equipment which makes every amateur a competent photographer (if there are any brains behind his eyes) it is hard for many people to comprehend the universal importance of the professional during the decades preceding the '90's. But remember that the Leica and even the simplest Kodak were still undreamed miracles. If you wanted a picture, you sat in a chair, put your head in a vise, watched the birdie, and laid your cash on the barrelhead. There wasn't any other way.[13]

The vise Jackson refers to was a clamp placed behind the subject to hold the head steady during the long exposure time. This was one reason why people look rather rigid in nineteenth century photographs. Another reason is given by John Carter, author of *Solomon D. Butcher: Photographing the American Dream:*

> The people Butcher photographed were intensely aware of the ability of the photograph to freeze time and in a sense provide immortality. . . . It is perhaps because of this respect for the image that people were seldom photographed in less than their best clothing. In fact, there are accounts of family members being excluded from family photographs because they did not own proper attire. [14]

Butcher's pictures have great value for scholars studying the process of settlement in the West. Over the sixteen years of the project, 1886-1901, the photographs show an evolution from the first hastily built soddies on the open prairie, where people and animals lived in cozy proximity, to larger, better constructed sod houses, barns and workshops, plowed and planted fields, fenced land, kitchen gardens, and corrals. Later came wood-frame houses with separate rooms (sod houses had no interior walls), yards, and flower gardens.

The publication of his *History* in 1901 brought Butcher success. The first edition of a thousand copies sold out immediately and a second thousand were ordered. He began to hatch plans for similar histories of the surrounding counties, but he could never raise enough money to carry out the projects. He did continue to photograph, however, and in 1904 he published *Sod Houses or the Development of the Great American Plains: A Pictorial History of the Men and Means That Have Conquered This Wonderful Country*. The title is revealing. It captures in a phrase two parallel feelings that many people held about the West: It was a wonderful country, yet it needed to be conquered.

As hard as he had worked, Butcher never made much money from his photography. Late in life he left the operation of his studio to his son Lynn and tried other schemes, including selling irrigated land in Texas and working as a traveling salesman for a grain and flour company.

His wish was to move to Texas to spend his last years in the Rio Grande Valley, but it would have been impossible for Butcher to haul his whole collection of some 3,000 full-plate glass negatives that far, simply because of their weight. So he tried to sell his collection to the

Nebraska Historical Society. The issue was debated in the Nebraska legislature, and finally resulted in an offer of the grand sum of $600. Butcher was not happy, but he accepted the offer. Unfortunately, however, his Texas land deals failed and he was forced to stay in Nebraska anyway. Later he complained, "My collection was worth $5,000.00 to the state, and if I had the collection now that I am going to stay in Nebraska they couldent [sic] buy them at any reasonable price."[15]

Butcher never did realize his dream of wealth for his family. He kept trying one scheme after another, including a patent medicine guaranteed to cure anything, which he advertised as BUTCHER'S WONDER OF THE AGE, and a device for detecting oil based on the technique of dowsing for water. As often happens, it was only after his death in 1927 that the value of Butcher's work was recognized. His collection is now featured at the Nebraska Historical Society and in the Library of Congress's American Memory project. Butcher's prints are widely used to illustrate history books, and they have been exhibited in prominent museums and galleries. Historians have come to recognize the value of his work to their research. Yet Solomon Butcher died poor, believing that no one appreciated the worth of what he had done.

CHAPTER SIX

The Many Faces of the American Indian

IN THE ROTUNDA of the Capitol building in Washington, D.C., there is a relief sculpture that was carved by the Italian artist Enrico Causici. It was commissioned by the United States government in 1827. The sculpture is titled *Daniel Boone Struggling with the Indian*. Squeezed into a narrow niche in the wall are Daniel Boone, frontier hero, and a fierce-looking Indian locked in hand-to-hand combat. The two figures are shown in profile. The sculpture commemorates an incident that occurred in 1773 when Boone was leading a group of settlers into Kentucky. They were attacked by Indians, but Daniel Boone's bravery roused the settlers to drive the Indians off.

What's noteworthy about this sculpture is the depiction of the Indian. His muscular body is clad only in a loincloth. Boone is fully clothed in his usual buckskins. The Indian is attacking with a tomahawk, which is poised to split Boone's skull. Boone is warding off the blow with his long rifle and holding a dagger in his other hand. But it is the Indian's face that is the most striking feature. It is distorted into a grotesque mask of savagery. His eyes bulge and his large nose and lower jaw are pinched together, throwing his features out of proportion and twisting his mouth into a snarl. A chain of some kind dangles from his ear, and feathers seem to sprout from the center of his shaved head. He is an altogether fearsome character.

Boone, on the other hand, is so calm and collected his handsome face looks as if he might be holding a friendly conversation rather than preparing to run the Indian through with his dagger.

Another view of the American Indian is represented in a group portrait done by Charles Bird King in 1821. It's a painting of a group of Pawnees who had come to Washington to negotiate with government officials. The Indians in this picture are handsome, their faces composed and calm, their features fine. Although they wear face paint and traditional clothing, there is nothing threatening about them. They show the opposite face of the American Indian from Causici's statue: They represent the Noble Savage of European myth.

The idea of the Noble Savage goes back to fifteenth-century Europe, when European explorers and travelers began to encounter non-white tribal people in various parts of the world. The exaggerated reports of some of these travelers painted native people as superior beings who had not been corrupted by civilization. From the sixteenth to the nineteenth centuries, hundreds of travel books were published, describing tribal societies in glowing terms. The Noble Savage, according to these accounts, lived a simpler, purer life under just and reasonable laws—a life of natural virtue, untainted by the oppression, greed, and selfishness that plagued western civilization.

These two views of the Indian, as noble savage and vicious beast, existed side by side in the minds of white Americans from the time of the first settlers. One or the other could be called up to serve whatever purpose was needed.

Through the 1830s and 40s the dominant image of the Indians was, in President Andrew Jackson's words, "savage bloodhounds." White settlement was rapidly spreading west from the eastern seaboard to the Mississippi valley. Settlers needed land and the Indians were in the way. Portraying the Indians as vicious animals, not really human, made it easier for the United States to embark on a policy of extermination. Fierce battles were fought, and many tribes were wiped out or reduced to a remnant. Those who remained fell prey to Jackson's brutal removal policy. In 1838 fifteen thousand Cherokee were forced to march from their lands in Georgia along the Trail of Tears to Indian Territory (present-day Oklahoma). For thousands, it was a death march. Jackson made no bones about it; he was a segregationist and wanted complete separation of whites and Indians, and he wanted Indian land.

Once the Indian population in the East had been reduced to the point where it was no threat at all, a new image of the Indian arose. It can be seen in an 1847 painting by Tompkins Harrison Matteson called *The Last of the Race*. The painting shows a group of four Indians gathered on a cliff facing the Pacific Ocean—the edge of the continent. It is sunset but dark clouds form a barrier on the horizon. There are two men, a chief in a red robe and a young man, and two women. Perhaps a family. The chief, standing, gazes out to sea while the dog looks up at him expectantly—but there is nowhere left to go. The two women are seated, one looking out to sea, the other back toward the land. The young man stands with his hands cupped over his rifle barrel, leaning on it, and his forehead resting on his hands. The painting is suffused with the weak light of the dying sun.

This is a sorrowful, sentimental picture, an example of Romanticism reduced to a sad, nostalgic melancholy. In the East, with towns turned into cities and wagons heading west, the Indians were neither Noble Savages nor vicious killers. They were a defeated people, no longer a real threat; therefore, whites could afford to feel sympathy for them. There is a feeling of loss about the painting, as though the decline of the Indian way of life had diminished the country in some way.

These various images of the Indian were well established in the minds of Americans when photography arrived, just in time to document the confrontation between whites and Indians in the West. The western experience added another layer of interpretation to the image of the Indian. As exploration advanced, some of the romantic mystique of the western lands carried over to the the Indian. As historian William H. Goetzmann explains,

> To most men of the day, the Indian was merely one of the many Western wonders—marvels, freaks, and exotics, all the more interesting because they

were sometimes dangerous. They were grass-skirted Mojaves, wretched dirt-daubed Diggers, Mokis from the painted-desert courts of Kubla Khan, Assiniboin buffalo hunters, implacable Sioux, Pueblo apartment-house dwellers. They were Navaho with their gaudy blankets, Comanche, centaurs of the plains and canyons, and Klickitats from the great north paddling carved war canoes fifty feet long. With few exceptions, they were to most observers, not men at all. In the 1850's they were not even an acute problem. They were marvels—the very symbol of romantic America.[1]

Much of the photography produced for the commercial market played to one or another of the stereotypes that cloaked the reality of the Indian. The reality was that throughout the nineteenth century, human beings were being either exterminated or herded onto reservations, living in miserable conditions. But as early as the 1860s the Plains Indians were already being romanticized as noble but doomed warriors or innocent children of nature—or simply curiosities. As tourism swelled during the 1870s, so did the vogue for Indian photographs, and many photographers who had little interest in Indians approached them in the same spirit as they would an unusual rock formation or a picturesque waterfall—grist for the tourist mill.

The U.S. government also used photography to further its policies. Photographs from the geological surveys and other expeditions, including pictures of western tribes, were widely published, exhibited, and sold. In addition, the government commissioned portraits of Indian delegations that visited Washington, D.C., usually to sign treaties giving up their land. These pictures depicted the Indians as tame and harmless, suggesting that the "Indian problem" was under control. If the Indians came to Washington dressed in suits and ties, as they often did, the photographers kept a supply of traditional buckskins and feathered headdresses in their studios. Individuals and groups were posed for portraits in ceremonial dress, usually holding a tomahawk or peace pipe. The photographs needed to fit the prevailing stereotypes.

Pictures of treaty signings, which showed the Indians as peaceful, were very popular with the public. In 1867, William S. Soule pho-

An engraving from a photograph by Alexander Gardner, printed in *Harper's Weekly*, 1867. An Indian delegation at Washington, D.C. is making a presentation to the president, probably Andrew Johnson. The Indians are dressed in traditional costumes, in sharp contrast to the formal wear of the whites. Courtesy of the Denver Public Library, Western History Collection, X-33768.

tographed the signing of the Medicine Lodge Treaty in Kansas. This was an important treaty between the U.S. government and several of the Plains tribes that restricted the Indians to reservations and cleared the way for the Union Pacific Railroad. Soule immediately sent the negatives to his brother in New York, who copyrighted them and did a brisk business hawking copies. In another instance, in 1886, Gen. George Crooks asked the photographer Camillus Fly to photograph the surrender of the once-threatening Apache chief Geronimo in Mexico. Fly accepted the offer. The picture, which was published in

Harper's Weekly, became immediately famous and sold well in the East.

There were some efforts during the last half of the nineteenth century to use photography to produce a more objective record of Indian life than posed and dressed-up portraits. Human cultures were becoming subjects for scientific study within the budding field of ethnography. As early as 1865, the first secretary of the Smithsonian Institution, Joseph Henry, urged "a far more authentic and trustworthy collection of likenesses of the principal tribes of the U.S. . . . The Indians are passing away so rapidly that but few years remain within which this can be done and the loss will be irretrievable and so felt when they are gone."[2] In the same spirit, the expeditions that went out under the banner of the U.S. Geological Survey were charged with documenting Indian life as part of their scientific study of the land. And the photographers who accompanied these expeditions made thousands of photographs. They photographed villages, and individuals and groups in their natural settings.

There is always an element of the subjective in a photograph, however. One telling example of this can be found in the diary of William Henry Jackson when he was with the Hayden survey in the 1870s. After an unsuccessful day searching for ancient cliff dwellings rumored to exist in the Mesa Verde region of Colorado, he wrote this: "Had found nothing that really came up to my idea of the grand or picturesque for photos and began to feel a little doubtful and discouraged." Jackson, like everyone else, carried with him the preconceptions of his culture, and his ideas of what was suitable or interesting could color his choice of subject matter. The next day Jackson was happier when the party came upon a house perched impossibly high on a plateau: "There it was," he wrote, "a marvel and a puzzle."[3]

The work of the survey photographers left a valuable record of Indian life, but the local photographers who lived and worked in western towns also contributed a great deal. Because they were permanent residents, some of them were able to form close relationships with the nearby tribes. Of course, there were plenty who exploited the Indians for their own gain, but there were also those who had a genuine interest in these people and earned their affection and respect.

Typical of photographers whose interest in Indians was mainly commercial was David F. Barry. He began his photographic career in 1878 in Bismarck, North Dakota, and between 1878 and 1883 he traveled throughout Dakota Territory and into eastern Montana photographing forts and battlefields of the Plains Indian wars, as well as soldiers, trappers, and other western characters. But he made his mark with portraits of famous Indians. In a magazine article about Sitting Bull, which used some of Barry's photographs, Barry is identified as "Photographer of Noted Indians."

Most of Barry's pictures are formal studio portraits. He took a portable gallery along on his travels, and the pictures show considerable attention given to dress, props, and posing. Sometimes Barry poses himself with his Indian subjects. His portraits, with his subjects most often outfitted in elaborate ceremonial garb, were obviously staged to appeal to the public's desire for the exotic and romantic. However, Barry did produce some powerful pictures, like his portraits of Sitting Bull, Rain in the Face, and Red Cloud, which convey a strong sense of character. But much of his work looks contrived and overly dramatic. And sometimes, even bizarre—like the picture of Hairy Chin dressed in an Uncle Sam suit and holding an umbrella.

More in the spirit of authentic documentary photography was the work of Horace Poley of Colorado Springs who arrived in Colorado in the 1880s. In addition to commercial work, he produced a large body of photographs documenting the life of his community—scenic views, parades and public celebrations, mining and miners, prospectors with burros. But he is best known for his photography of the Indian communities in the Southwest.

During summer vacations, Poley photographed for archaeological expeditions to Arizona, New Mexico, Utah, and southwestern Colorado. As a regular visitor to these places, he was allowed a more

Barry's Photographic Studio (c. 1898) by David F. Barry. In this studio and gallery in Superior, Wisconsin, David Barry displayed framed photographs, Indian artifacts, and props used in photographic work. Courtesy of the Denver Public Library, Western History Collection, B-783.

intimate view of Indian life than would a traveler just passing through. He was able to gain the people's trust, and as a result his photographs have the feel of candid glimpses of people going about their daily business. In a letter to the Denver Public Library in 1935, Poley wrote that he possessed, among other things, many pictures of the Ute Indians, "as my acquaintance with these Indians gave me unusual oppertunity [sic] for photographing them."[4]

Poley became well known in his city as a lecturer on Indian life, and he used photographs to illustrate his lectures. These pictures were made into transparencies and projected with an early form of slide projector called a "magic lantern." To enhance the realism of his slides, Poley hand-colored many of them.

During the closing decades of the nineteenth century, photographers were helped along by some major technical improvements which transformed the nature of photography. One was the development of a dry plate to replace the old messy wet-plate process. As early as 1867, dry plates using the same collodion emulsion as the old wet plates were being produced. These plates worked but were not sensitive enough for practical photography. Then in 1871, a doctor named Richard Maddox wrote a letter to the *British Journal of Photography* describing a process he had developed using a gelatin emulsion. Maddox didn't have time to continue his experiments, but others improved his process until, in 1879, a fast dry plate was successfully produced.

These new plates were so good that pictures could be taken without a tripod. The camera could now be held in the hand. This was a revolutionary development in the history of photography. It produced a flood of hand cameras in the 1880s. Some of them held magazines of a dozen or more plates, so that the photographer didn't have to reload after every exposure. Then came the novelty items—cameras disguised as packages, suitcases, books, and watches; cameras that could be hidden in hats or behind neckties. But nothing changed photography as much as the Kodak, introduced by its inventor George Eastman in 1888. This was the camera that finally brought photography to the masses.

George Eastman distinguished two kinds of amateur photographers: serious amateurs those who worked with care and took the trouble to learn their craft, and the casual snapshooters whose interest in the techniques of photography extended no further than the location of the button on their cameras.

One of the best of the serious amateurs, Adam Clark Vroman, worked among the Pueblo tribes of the Southwest between 1895 and 1904. He was dedicated to recording accurately and respectfully these unique cultures. Vroman preferred the traditional large view camera over the smaller hand camera for its ability to capture greater richness of detail. However, swarms of Kodak-toting tourists descending in large numbers on the American Indians caused problems that earlier field

THE KODAKING OF AMERICA

When asked where he got the name Kodak, George Eastman said he just made it up; he wanted a word that would be short, pronounce-able in any language, distinctive, and easy to remember. In his youth Eastman started out as an amateur wet-plate photographer but found the process too complicated. After three years' experimentation in his mother's kitchen, he had developed a dry-plate formula and bought a factory to make the plates. Eastman's goal was, as he put it, "To make the camera as convenient as a pencil."

The first Kodaks came loaded with what Eastman called "American film," which was a roll of paper coated with a gelatin emulsion. The camera held enough film for 100 pictures. When all of the film was exposed, the camera was sent back to the factory. Then the film was developed and printed, and the camera was reloaded and returned to the owner for another 100 pictures.

These inventions, along with improvements in cameras and lenses, ushered in the age of amateur photography. "You push the but-ton and we do the rest" proclaimed the motto of the Eastman-Kodak Company. Now anyone could take a photograph and practically every-one did. The tourist armed with a camera, snapping away at every-thing in sight, became a standard feature of the western landscape.

photographers didn't have to face. Vroman complained that there were so many snapshooters the Indians were getting skittish around cameras. Because of this, Vroman had to get to know his subjects and gain their confidence before he could take thoughtful pictures. This turned out to be an advantage, for it gave a more personal touch to his photographs. He explained his approach in an article in *Photo Era* magazine in 1901:

> If you are a little patient, and do not try to hurry matters you will have but little trouble in getting what you want. The Indian must always have plenty of time to think over anything he has to do, and you cannot rush

Nampeyo's Daughter and Her Child (1901) by Adam Clark Vroman. There is a strong feeling of connection between the photographer and his subject in this portrait. Courtesy of the Seaver Center for Western History Research, Los Angeles County Museum of Natural History.

him a particle; sit down with him, show him the camera inside and out, stand on your head (on the ground-glass) for him, or anything you want him to do, and he will do the same for you.[5]

The reference to "stand on your head" refers to the fact that the image on the ground glass of a view camera appears upside down. Vroman is saying that he let his subject view him through the camera.

For nine years, Vroman traveled from his home in California to Arizona and New Mexico to photograph the Hopi, Navajo, and Zuni people. He was a sympathetic and knowledgeable observer, genuinely interested in the people and their culture, and his work has been widely praised for its care and respectfulness.

∾

IN 1890, THE MASSACRE of Sioux Indians at Wounded Knee ended the Indian wars, and in the same year the U.S. Census Bureau declared the frontier closed. The Census Bureau report said that there was no longer a line—a frontier—separating settled land from wilderness. The age of the Indian freely roaming the Plains was over. Indians were either packed into reservations or put to work re-enacting famous battles with Buffalo Bill's Wild West Show. The Wild West retreated further, through story and film, into the haze of the American imagination.

Photography had advanced and the Wild West had faded away. Together these developments worked a transformation in the image of the Indian in the West much like the transformation that had happened over half a century ago in the East. The Indian as romantic symbol of a dying way of life became the dominant theme at the same time as documentary studies were trying to preserve authentic evidence of it. At times, the two impulses operated simultaneously, making it difficult in a photograph to untangle one motive from the other.

In 1909 the photographer Joseph Dixon went to photograph on the Crow reservation in Montana. He was sponsored by Redman Wanamaker, son of the owner of Wanamaker department stores in Philadelphia and New York. Wanamaker had arranged a series of "Expeditions to the American Indian" headed by Dixon. The year before, Dixon had made a film of Henry Wadsworth Longfellow's poem *The Song of Hiawatha* using Indians from the reservation. It didn't seem to matter at this point in history that Hiawatha was from an eastern Iroquois tribe, not the western Crow. On his second trip, Dixon attended the second annual Crow fair, and he also photographed survivors of the battle of the Little Bighorn at the site of the battle. Then finally, he assembled a group of about fifty chiefs from several tribes to stage what he called *The Last Great Indian Council*. Afterwards, he had them ride over a hilltop while he photographed them.

Dixon had a particular idea in mind of what he wanted to accomplish with this photograph. He was after something more than a group

Sunset of a Dying Race (1909) by
Joseph Dixon. The original negative here shows a group of Indians
riding over a hill. The final image,
doctored by Dixon, showcases a
lone warrior riding into the sunset.
Courtesy of William Hammond
Mathers Museum, Indiana
University.

of Indians riding over the hill, so he made a couple of adjustments when he printed the negative. First, he made an overlay that blocked out all but one of the figures, a lone Indian on horseback. Next, by darkening parts of the sky and adding cloud effects from another negative, he made it appear that the figure was riding off into a dramatic sunset. Thus a fairly straightforward picture became an emotionally charged image meant to arouse feelings of sadness and sympathy for a people whose traditional way of life was fast disappearing. Dixon called this picture *The Sunset of a Dying Race*. Once again the American Indian became a romantic symbol for a vanishing past.

To evoke such feelings in viewers, Dixon sometimes manipulated images in other ways as well. He controlled the way his portrait subjects appeared in order to give an impression of times past. For instance, by the early twentieth century most Indians had adopted the clothing of white Americans—except for ceremonial occasions. However, Dixon only published portraits of Indians dressed in traditional garb and placed in a setting free of any modern objects. Although this sort of thing was common practice among photographers exploiting Indians for profit, Dixon was not an unscrupulous operator. He had great sympathy for the Indian and worked hard for a variety of Indian causes. He worked for the civil rights of Indians, and in the summer of 1909 he and his staff traveled to over 150 reservations across the country in an effort to gain citizenship for those Indians who were not yet American citizens. He continued his interest in Indian affairs through World War I, documenting Native Americans in the military.

Chapter Seven

Saving Shadows
The Indian Photography of Edward S. Curtis

By far the most ambitious project to photograph Indian life in the early twentieth century was undertaken by Edward S. Curtis. Curtis was born in Whitewater, Wisconsin, in 1868. As a teenager, he learned the basics of photography on his own, with the aid of self-help guides. At the age of nineteen he moved with his family to Seattle, in Washington Territory. His father died soon after, and Curtis suddenly found himself responsible for supporting his mother and his younger brother and sister. He took whatever work he could find—farming, fishing, digging clams—and managed to scrape together enough money to buy a camera. In 1891 he bought a share in a photographic gallery for $150, and a year later set up his own gallery.

Curtis immediately began photographing the native peoples of the Northwest Coast. One of his first Indian portraits was of Princess Angeline, daughter of Chief Sealth, for whom the city of Seattle was named. In 1899 Curtis won a first place prize at the National Photographic Convention for three of his pictures of Northwest Indians, and he joined the Harriman Expedition to Alaska. It would be the last great exploratory expedition of the nineteenth century. Like other photographers, Curtis took pictures of scientific and commercial interest—the land, the glaciers, plant and animal life. The expedition came back with over 5,000 photographs and specimens of 600 species of plants and animals that scientists had never seen. Curtis also took the opportunity to photograph the Indians of the far north. He struck up a friendship with another member of the expedition, an ethnologist named Robert Grinnel who was an expert on Native American cultures. Curtis learned a great deal from him.

These experiences led Curtis to conceive a grand project. He saw that the way of life of tribes he worked with was on the verge of extinction. Ancient traditions and customs were fast disappearing. Curtis decided to preserve what he could of Indian life in photographs. To accomplish this, he committed himself to photographing every single group of Indians west of the Mississippi. It was a grand scheme, one that would occupy thirty years of his life

The result was a massive, twenty-volume collection called *The North American Indian*. This work contains more than 2,200 photographs from over eighty tribes in the United States and Canada. Curtis also collected stories and songs from the tribes he visited and kept extensive ethnographic notes about customs, work, ceremonies, tribal organization, family relationships, arts and crafts, and everyday life. It was an expensive project, and Curtis had to spend much of his time seeking funding. His first efforts were financed by Doubleday publishers, but it was not enough support.

Curtis exhibited his work in many galleries in the East and in Seattle, building a reputation. His work impressed President Theodore Roosevelt, who asked him to photograph the Apache warrior Geronimo and five other Indian chiefs on the lawn of the White House. Curtis also photographed the president with his family. Roosevelt became a strong supporter. In 1906, he introduced Curtis to the financier J.P. Morgan, who paid the photographer $75,000 to support the venture. When the first volume of *The North American Indian* was published in 1907, the *New York Herald* newspaper praised it as "the most gigantic undertaking in the making of books since the King James edition of the Bible."

Today Curtis is most famous for his posed portraits, but he also included in his project many pictures of daily life— preparing food and

Snake Dancers Entering the Plaza (c.1921) by Edward S. Curtis. Curtis's description of this photo of Hopi snake dancers is an example of the kind of ethnographic information he collected. He wrote, "At the right stand the Antelopes, in front of the booth containing the snake-jars. The Snakes enter the plaza, encircle it four times with military tread, and then after a series of songs remarkable for their irresistible movement, they proceed to dance with the reptiles." Courtesy of The McCormick Library of Special Collections, Northwestern University Library.

cooking, weaving and making pottery, family gatherings and children's games. Because he treated people with respect, Curtis was also allowed to photograph special ceremonies, like the sun dance of the Blackfeet of Montana, that white people usually were not permitted to see.

Over the years, Morgan continued to support Curtis with grants. But the project kept growing, year after year, so Curtis had to pay much of the expense himself. He not only had to pay for his materials and printing, but also for a team of assistants to help with the work. When volume 20 was finally published in 1930, Curtis was divorced, broke, and in poor health. His North American Indian Company had gone bankrupt. The final cost of the project was $1.5 million.

Curtis spared no expense in printing his book. The twenty volumes of *The North American Indian* were painstakingly printed on hand-operated presses using a new process called *photogravure*. It's a time-consuming and expensive process, and Curtis insisted on the finest materials—the highest quality paper available and Moroccan leather binding. The prints he made are exceptionally beautiful, having a richness of tone rarely matched in the history of photographic printing.

Curtis had hoped to sell 500 copies at $3,000 each but was able to raise subscriptions for only a little over half that number. Public interest in the American Indian dwindled during World War I and the Great Depression of the 1930s, and Curtis's work was all but forgotten. His negatives and plates were taken by his creditors and disappeared until 1977, when they were found boxed and stored in a used book shop in Boston.

～

IN 1999, THE Hockaday Museum of Art in Kalispell, Montana, mounted an exhibition of Edward Curtis's photographs titled *Images of an Idyllic Past*. This title captures the particular way in which Curtis imagined his project. The word "idyllic" suggests a romantic view of the past, a view of a simpler, happier time—which is exactly what Curtis had set out to do. In the introduction to *The North American Indian* he wrote that his aim was to photograph all of the tribes that "still retain to a considerable degree their primitive customs and traditions." [1]

For most American Indians in the early years of the twentieth century, present reality boiled down to two choices: live a life of poverty on a reservation or become a part of white society. It was the position of the Bureau of Indian Affairs that Native Americans would have to give up their old ways and adapt to society if they were going to survive. The U.S. government pressured them for years to change their ways. Some tribes were forced to settle down and become farmers, even though traditionally they had been nomadic hunters. Indian children were sent to schools where their native languages were forbidden and they were forced to behave and dress like white children. Indians who had roamed the land freely were confined to reservations, often in appalling conditions. Like many other Americans Curtis's feelings about the Indian were mixed: He agreed with the Bureau of Indian Affairs that Indians would have to change, but at the same time he regretted the passing of a way of life.

Since its rediscovery in 1977, Curtis's work has attracted a great deal of attention. His photographs have touched off spirited discussion and controversy. Most of the controversy is over the charge that Curtis manipulated his images to create a false, romanticized picture of Indian life.

By his own admission, Curtis's purpose was to preserve the past, and it is true that he controlled details in his photographs to create an impression of time gone by. For example, the first photograph in *The North American Indian* is of a Navajo band riding through a canyon on horseback. The slant of the light suggests sunset, and the Indians are riding into it. The picture recalls Joseph Dixon's *Sunset of a Dying Race*, which is echoed in Curtis's title, *The Vanishing Race*. While the picture itself may not have been manipulated, the title imposes a certain interpretation on it. In his introduction, Curtis wrote about this photograph, "The thought that this picture is meant to convey is that the Indians as a race, already shorn of their tribal strength and stripped

The Vanishing Race (c. 1904) by Edward S. Curtis. Courtesy of The McCormick Library of Special Collections, Northwestern University Library.

of their primitive dress, are passing into the darkness of an unknown future." This theme of the Vanishing Race appeared frequently in American art and photography, as it did in the painting of Tompkins Matteson, discussed earlier, and in the photography of Joseph Dixon. By the late nineteenth century this perception of the Indian as a tragic primitive on the verge of extinction was widespread in white America. The general feeling was that it was a shame it had to happen, but there was really no other way. Manifest destiny had made it inevitable. As the journalist Horace Greely had declared after an overland trip to California back in 1859, "These people must die out, there is no help for them." This feeling was found not only in photographs and paintings, but in the magazines and newspapers of the time. It could be seen in the brisk business conducted in postcards and artifacts, and in cheap prints of Indian chiefs, medicine men, and warriors. Edward Curtis was undoubtedly influenced by this view of the Indian. It was all around him.

Curtis controlled his photographs more explicitly in ways that had become the stock in trade of many western photographers. Clothing is one of the key indicators of historical time in any image of people. Among Curtis's most popular pictures are portraits of Indian people in traditional clothes—feather headdresses, buckskins, bead necklaces. Sometimes the captions for these photos suggest that this was everyday wear. The fact is that most Indians in the early twentieth century wore pretty much what other Americans were wearing. But an Indian in a suit or a pair of pants and cotton shirt would hardly have aroused feelings of a romantic past. If the right clothing wasn't available, Curtis sometimes designed or supplied it himself, even providing wigs if his subjects had cut their hair.

Curtis was also careful to avoid including modern articles in his portraits, even though Indians had readily adopted what was useful or pleasing to them from white American culture—tools and materials for building and carving, hunting and fishing, cooking and making clothing. But these things could not be allowed in a photograph. Axes, parasols, suspenders, frying pans, guns—all had to be removed. And if an offending object had been accidentally included, it would be gone before the picture was printed. One negative, for example, shows that great care was taken to scratch out an alarm clock.

Another clue to historical time is setting. When Curtis photographed his subjects outdoors, he usually placed them in settings that suggested unspoiled nature, free of the trappings of civilization—the American Eden that existed before European contact. No automobiles in the background or telegraph wires running across the sky. He sometimes also placed objects in the picture that the Indians themselves hadn't used for many years. At times Curtis had his subjects reenact old battle scenes or put on ritual dances just for the camera. In these pictures he was careful to eliminate anything that would indicate modern time.

Edward Curtis had an idea of what he wanted to achieve, and he had no qualms about adjusting reality to achieve it. According to the code of modern journalism, this would be considered dishonest. But Curtis was a man of his time, and few people would have seen anything wrong with the way he worked. Today there are Native Americans who praise Curtis for preserving reminders of their old traditions and customs. His pictures are even collected in tribal archives. And it should also be noted that not all of Curtis's photographs were manipulated. Among his 40,000 negatives there are many that faithfully record Indians as they were living at the time.

It was not only current attitudes toward the Indian that influenced Curtis. A movement in photography that was gathering followers during the early twentieth century also played a part. This movement was called *pictorialism.* The pictorialists sought to establish photography as an art on a par with painting and drawing. To do that, they believed, the "real" photographers had to be separated from the thousands of amateurs out there clicking away with their Kodaks. A plain photograph wasn't good enough. It had to be "art," and art had to do more than that.

The pictorialists claimed that the main appeal of an "artistic" photograph should be to the emotions. Visual accuracy, they declared, was not important—in fact, too much visual accuracy was "inartistic." Unfortunately, the camera is the paragon of visual accuracy. So the pictorialists used a variety of techniques to make their photographs look as little as possible like photographs and as much as possible like paintings or lithographs. They began to draw and paint and scratch on their negatives. One of their favorite techniques was to throw the camera a little bit out of focus for a blurred effect because a clear, sharp picture was too much like . . . well . . . a photograph! Blurring the natural sharpness of a photograph suited well the emotional effect most in vogue at that time—a kind of hazy, romantic nostalgia. Country people leading a peaceful life in harmony with nature was a favored theme.

The pictorial movement reached its peak in the United States in the late nineteenth and early twentieth centuries, but it had been underway for some time in Europe. In 1858, the British photographer Henry Peach Robinson wrote an article promoting artificiality in photographs. He said, "Any 'dodge, trick, and conjuration' of any kind is open to the photographer's use. . . . It is his imperative duty to avoid the mean, the bare and the ugly, and to aim to elevate his subject, to avoid awkward forms, and to correct the unpicturesque. . . . A great deal can be done and very beautiful pictures made, by a mixture of the real and the artificial in a picture." Robinson went much further than Curtis ever did in controlling the details in his pictures; for example, he would pose models dressed up as country folk in his gallery, then combine parts of several negatives to make the final print.

Edward Curtis was very much aware of these trends and must have been swayed by them. He used such pictorialist techniques as fading light, soft focus effects, and dramatic contrasts of shadows and highlights to enhance the feeling of nostalgia. But this tendency was only one side of Curtis. Many of his portraits of individuals are direct, powerful character studies, free of any manipulation except, perhaps, costume. Curtis was an amateur ethnographer with a romantic bent, and

*Chief Raven Blanket—
Nez Perce* (c.1910) by
Edward S. Curtis. A
posed portrait of a chief
in full ceremonial
regalia. Courtesy of The
McCormick Library of
Special Collections,
Northwestern University
Library.

the two strands are tightly intertwined in his work. His ethnographic
side comes out most clearly in his many close studies of faces. In a few
cases, the subjects are named, but most of them are simply labeled with
the name of their tribe—Navajo woman, Blackfoot warrior. Some captions, like *Quinault Female Type*, even indicate that Curtis was collect-
ing samples of certain human specimens for the scientific record.
Sometimes, Curtis took two head shots of the subject, one frontal and
one in profile, like mug shots. In a typical example, to pictures of an old
man, the photographs are labeled *Klickitat Type* and *Klickitat Profile*,
nothing more.

After the publication of his great book, Curtis continued to work as a gallery photographer. He also spent some time in Los Angeles assisting in the movie industry. In 1920, he had worked with Cecil B. DeMille on the filming of *The Ten Commandments*, and he had made a couple of films of his own about North American Indians. During the 1940s, he planned another mammoth project on the subject of gold mining, but it was never completed. In 1952, Edward Curtis died of a heart attack in Los Angeles.

The Indian has been given many faces in American art and photography. These faces often reflected the deep-seated beliefs and fears and desires of white America more than they did the people in front of the camera. If the Indians needed to be removed from the land, they were given one face; when they were gone, another face cloaked the act in a romantic haze. What was lost among all of these masks was the human face. As William Goetzmann points out in *Exploration and Empire*, "With few exceptions, they were to most observers, not men at all."

Chapter Eight

The Last of the Great Frontier Photographers

WILLIAM HENRY JACKSON did more than any other photographer to shape America's image of the West. He produced thousands of photographs from nine years working with the U.S. Geological Survey and from his own businesses in Omaha and Denver. He was there with his camera at the beginning of the great western expansion that followed the Civil War, and he was there when the U.S. Census Bureau announced in 1890 that the frontier was officially closed. His work spans, from beginning to end, those legendary years in American history we think of as the Old West.

Jackson left not only an immense photographic legacy, but he also wrote a great deal about his life and work. He kept detailed diaries, and in his late nineties published his autobiography, *Time Exposure*. As a result, we have from Jackson a fuller picture of a photographer's life during those years than from any other source.

There was little in Jackson's early life to suggest the kind of man he would become. When the war ended in 1865, he was working as a retoucher in a photographic gallery in Burlington, Vermont. He was spending his days removing warts and blemishes from portraits, making people look better than they really did. As a boy, Jackson had taught himself to draw and paint and he was skilled with a brush. After serving out a three-year enlistment in the Union army, he was settling into a comfortable life in Burlington, joining the art and literary societies and acting in amateur plays. He was engaged to be married. As he wrote in *Time Exposure*, "I liked things as they were in 1866."[1] He was twenty-four years old.

Then everything changed. It was a broken engagement over what Jackson called a "difference" with his fiancee that caused him to give up the settled life and move on. "I found it impossible in my shame to face the world," he wrote. The next day he left for New York. In the city he met an old friend from the army, who talked Jackson into going west to find work with one of the silver mining companies in Montana Territory. Within a week Jackson was on a train headed for Detroit.

As it turned out, Jackson never made it to Montana. Short of cash, he worked his way west by picking up odd jobs. In St. Joseph, Missouri, he found work as a bullwhacker driving an ox-drawn wagon in a Mormon wagon train heading for Salt Lake City. For the next two years, Jackson knocked around the West doing various odd jobs. He worked as a wrangler and guard on wagon trains, and as a farmhand and carpenter. In Utah, he tutored art students. Finally, in 1868 he settled in Omaha, Nebraska, and opened his first photography gallery.

But Jackson found that he was not cut out to be a gallery photographer, stuck indoors posing people for portraits all day. He had developed a taste for the outdoors. So he brought his brother in to take charge of the gallery while he spent most of his time wandering and photographing in the surrounding country. He discovered that there was a growing demand in the East for western photographs, both of the land and of the native people, so every now and then he went out for a few days to photograph among the local tribes. In *Time Exposure* he recalled, "They [the Indians] were all friendly–and there was money there, both for the red man and the photographer. Those Indians would pose for me by the hour for small gifts of cash, or just for tobacco or a knife or an old waistcoat. And I in turn was able to sell the pictures through local outlets and by way of dealers in the East."

Jackson never could manage to stay home for very long. Even when he married in 1869, he took off on a long trip of his own after a honeymoon of only six days. He was drawn by the excitement over the just-completed transcontinental railroad. "The thing that really got to me was the railroad. Here was something truly earth-shaking, and, whether or not there had been a dime in it for me, sooner or later I would have been out on the grade with my cameras." Jackson and a friend rode the railroad from Omaha to Salt Lake City. They didn't have much money, so they worked out a clever scheme to finance their trip: At each town along the way they would stop and set up a temporary portrait business until they had earned enough money to buy tickets to the next town. Along the way, Jackson also photographed settlements and, as he put it, "all the striking natural views of the surrounding country."

On this trip, Jackson honed his skills as a landscape photographer. He also learned a few things about the business of photography. On the way out of Cheyenne, Wyoming, the train boy bought all of Jackson's Indian pictures and ordered a thousand stereoscopic views of Weber Canyon to sell to tourists. Clearly, eastern tourists were willing to plunk down good money for mementos of the West.

Jackson's pictures from this trip are more than dutiful records of scenery. The photographer brought to his work certain ideas and feelings about the West, nature, and national purpose. Like most white Americans he was simultaneously dazzled by the raw natural beauty of the landscape and excited by the building of the railroad. One of Jackson's great talents throughout his career was his ability to reconcile these often-conflicting views. His pictures preserve a sense of the grandeur of unspoiled nature at the same time as they depict the human presence as benign. They suggest you can have it both ways.

Jackson took a number of pictures of railroad workers on this trip, making a little traveling money by selling the men copies. Typically in these pictures, the men are small, dwarfed by the monumental scale of the landscape. The message is that nature is the greater power. And yet the work of these men–the tracks they lay and the bridges they build–demonstrates that they are up to the challenge of this wild country. And finally, Jackson has composed the pictures in such a way that the trains and tracks and trestles don't seem out of place. They look like an integral part of the landscape, a welcome sign of human presence and a civilizing force. Most often the tracks are slanting off into the distance, a dynamic diagonal, suggesting the forward drive of progress. In these pictures the viewer can feel that the conflicts have been resolved, that conquering nature doesn't mean despoiling it. In his future work, Jackson refined this ability to harmonize differing views of the land.

"I returned to Omaha late in September," Jackson wrote, "with just about the finest assortment of negatives that had yet come out of the West." He stayed home and worked in his studio until the summer of 1870, when he received a visit from Ferdinand Hayden, leader of an expedition sent by the United States Geologic and Geographical Survey of the Territories to explore the West. Hayden was returning to Wyoming when he called on Jackson. He needed a photographer for the expedition, and he had been impressed by Jackson's work of the previous summer. It was a visit that set Jackson on the next phase of his career. As he recalled,

> [Hayden] spent a long time studying my Union Pacific pictures and the Indian groups I had photographed near Omaha. Then, with a sigh, he remarked, "This is what I need. I wish I could offer you enough to make it worth your while to spend the summer with me."
>
> "What *could* you offer?" I asked quickly.
>
> "Only a summer of hard work–and the satisfaction I think you would find in contributing your art to science. Of course, all your expenses would be paid, but . . ."

Two days later, Jackson was on his way to Cheyenne, without pay. It was an opportunity to photograph unexplored territory and to build himself a reputation. He wasn't as experienced as some of the other survey photographers, such as Timothy O'Sullivan or Alexander Gardner, and this was a chance to learn. Jackson learned well.

Hayden wanted to have Jackson along for reasons other than science. The United States Congress controlled the money to finance these expeditions, and there was considerable competition for it. At this time four major surveys were scouting the West. Each year they had to report to Congress to renew their funding. Congress wanted to see that these surveys were producing results, and it wanted to publicize the West to encourage settlement and tourism. Hayden knew that outstanding photographs of the scenery, the native people, and the survey at work would give him an advantage when it came time to give his report.

The job of survey photographer required a variety of abilities. Some of the work was straightforward documentation for scientific use: rock formations, plants, topography. These pictures had to be as objective as possible, taken from a point of view that showed most clearly the features that interested the scientists. They had to contain maximum detail and clarity. Another kind of work aimed at prying money out of Congress and attracting settlers and tourists. Here, artistic values became important. The photographer needed to choose views and compose the picture to accentuate the wild beauty of the place, but at the same time make the land look inviting. Jackson's ability to resolve conflicting views served this purpose well.

Jackson worked with the Hayden survey every summer from 1870 until it ended in 1878, and he steadily developed his craft. Survey work also brought him into contact with others who helped him cultivate his art. On his first trip, in 1870, Jackson became friends with the expedition's artist, an accomplished New York landscape painter named Sanford Gifford. The two of them often worked together. Gifford was an easterner inspired by Thomas Cole and the Hudson River School. He was associated with a group of painters called the Luminists, who used atmosphere and the play of light to create a sense of spirituality in nature. Gifford viewed landscape as the work of God, and he strove in his paintings to evoke a feeling of wonder at the grandeur of nature and, therefore, its creator. In his work, nature is vast and people, when they appear, are tiny. Still, there is a feeling of peace and serenity.

Gifford passed some of this knowledge along to Jackson. As a result, Jackson's photographs from the 1870 expedition appear more sophisticated than his earlier work. Ferdinand Hayden noticed the change. In the *Annual Report* for 1870 he wrote, "During the day Mr. Jackson, with the assistance of the fine artistic taste of Mr. Gifford, secured some most beautiful photographic views which will prove of great value to the artist as well as the geologist."[2] In the best of these views, the composition is carefully balanced and the sense of space more effectively rendered. Jackson often strategically placed members of the expedition in his photographs, and in the tradition of the eastern painters, human figures, camps, and settlements are tiny in relation to their surroundings. Although the figures represent the coming settlement of the land, it seems impossible that their kind could make much of a mark on such immense, measureless spaces. Often the figures are shown at rest, contemplating the splendor of the scene, as though inviting the viewer to see through their eyes.

The following year, 1871, Jackson's education continued when a well-known painter named Thomas Moran joined the survey. Like Gifford, Moran also sought the romantic and sublime in nature, but on a grander scale. Jackson and Moran struck up a lifelong friendship. As Jackson described the relationship, "Moran became greatly interested in photography, and it was my good fortune to have him at my side during all that season to help me solve many problems of composition. While learning a little from me, he was constantly putting in far more than he took out."

The artist and the photographer were together when the expedition visited the wilderness in Wyoming that would later become

---

Opposite page: *Lower Falls of the Yellowstone* (1871). Jackson took this photograph on his first trip to Yellowstone with the Hayden expedition. It is one of many pictures of these spectacular falls he made between 1871 and 1890. Barely visible, a man kneels on a rock in the lower left-hand corner. Courtesy Colorado Historical Society, neg. CHS-J1147, William Henry Jackson.

Yellowstone National Park. Tales of trappers and mountain men had been filtering back to the East for years, spreading rumors of a fantasy land of towering waterfalls and plunging canyons, of boiling mud springs and steaming geysers. It was known as "the place where hell bubbled up." Jackson was the first to photograph and Moran was the first to paint the wonders of Yellowstone.

Jackson's photographs of Yellowstone's spouting geysers and sulfurous hot springs held tremendous power to convince. Travelers could exaggerate and paintings could be manipulated, but here were actual photographs, real as a fingerprint, stamped by the direct action of light: The way things *really* looked. Publishers in the East raced to make engravings of these pictures to be printed in newspapers and magazines; copies of them hung in railroad offices and hotels, and adorned travel brochures. The camera, it was generally believed, did not lie.

These pictures, along with Moran's paintings, reached Washington, D.C. that winter just as the Senate was debating a bill introduced by Senator Samuel Clark Pomeroy of Kansas to make Yellowstone a national park. Pomeroy had presented the bill before, but there hadn't been much interest among the members. This time, he announced to the Senate, "There are photographs of the valley and the curiosities, which the Senators can see." The vote was unanimous. On March 1, 1872, President Ulysses S. Grant signed the bill into law, and Yellowstone became the first national park in the United States.

Dealing with the incredible, otherworldly landscape of Yellowstone was a photographic challenge in itself for Jackson. Moran's diary reveals that he and Jackson spent a good deal of time just looking for the best viewpoints. "Sketched but little," Moran wrote, "but worked hard with the photographer selecting points to be taken etc." And another time, "Went to the Geysers. Helped Jackson during the day and returned by myself to camp."[3] The best of Jackson's pictures from this trip show that he has mastered the painter's lessons well.

The fact that these men worked closely together offers interesting comparisons between painting and photography. Moran's most famous work from the Hayden expedition was a huge painting called *The Grand Canyon of the Yellowstone*. It measured eight feet by fourteen feet, and it caused a sensation when it was exhibited in the East. Congress finally bought it for $10,000, a lot of money in those days, and it was placed in the Senate lobby. Moran's commentary on this painting reveals his philosophy of the relationship between nature and art. He wrote,

> My general scope is not realistic; all my tendencies are toward idealization. . . . The motive or incentive of my "Grand Canyon of the Yellowstone" was the gorgeous display of color that impressed itself upon me. Probably no scenery in the world presents such a combination. The forms are extremely wonderful and pictorial, and, while I desired to tell truly of Nature, I did not wish to realize the scene literally, but to preserve and to convey its true impression.[4]

There is no physical place from which the view represented in Moran's painting actually can be seen. He assembled *The Grand Canyon of the Yellowstone* from his own sketches and Jackson's photographs after he returned to New York. He relied on the photographs for visual accuracy, but he said that his purpose was to convey the strongest possible impression, and he would do whatever he needed to do to accomplish that.

> Every form introduced into the picture is within view from a given point, but the relations of the separate parts to one another are not always preserved. For instance, the precipitous rocks on the right were really at my back when I stood at that point, yet in their present position they are strictly true to pictorial nature; and so correct is the whole representation that every member of the expedition with which I was connected declared, when he saw the painting, that he knew the exact spot which had been reproduced. My aim was to bring before the public the character of that region. The rocks in the foreground are so carefully drawn that a geologist could determine their precise nature.[5]

Grand Canyon of the Yellowstone (1872) by Thomas Moran. The painting that made Moran's reputation. It hung in the Senate lobby in the Capitol until 1950, when it was moved to its present home in the Department of the Interior Museum. Courtesy of the U.S. Department of the Interior Museum.

Moran represented the freedom of the painter to alter reality in service of what he saw as a greater truth. For landscape photographers like William Henry Jackson, the means of control are the basic elements of photography itself: choice of camera angle, lighting, and time of day, as well as decisions about what to include in the frame and what features to emphasize. Placing the camera high above a scene, for instance, heightens the feeling of vast open space. Choice of lens, too, can alter the depiction of space, making it look compressed and shallow or open and deep. Jackson became masterful at using such techniques to create the desired effect.

Painters in the West often used spectacular skies, especially flaming sunsets or rays of light bursting through billowing clouds, to suggest the glory of nature and the presence of the divine. This device was not available to photographers in the nineteenth century, nor was the use of color. The black-and-white emulsions photographers used could rarely record clouds; they were much more sensitive to blue light than to other colors, which meant that anything blue–like the sky–would print as white. Therefore, it was almost impossible to take a photograph properly exposed both for the land and the sky. Skies in nineteenth-century photographs tend to be blank white spaces. The photographer had to find other ways of dramatizing the power of nature.

Jackson often compensated for this lack by searching for dramatic details in the foreground and positioning his camera to take advantage of them, almost eliminating the sky. A low point of view combined with rocks or trees in the foreground strengthens the sense of place and draws the viewer closer to the scene. When his pictures do include expanses of sky, the white space is used to suggest the infinite expanse beyond the horizon.

Many of Jackson's photographs speak directly to the American ideal of nature as a source of divine power and spiritual renewal. One of his most celebrated pictures was a view of a mountain in the Rockies called the Mount of the Holy Cross. Lying down one slope of the mountain, two ravines filled with snow form the shape of a giant crucifix. The poet Henry Wadsworth Longfellow was moved by the picture to write these lines, from the sonnet "The Cross of Snow" (1879):

> There is a mountain in the distant West
> That, sun-defying, in its deep ravines
> Displays a cross of snow upon its side.

Jackson spent a good deal of the summer of 1873 deep within the Rockies searching for this legendary mountain. From tales of those who had seen it, it had become famous as an emblem of the divine in nature, and Jackson took some pains to strengthen that impression. On the negative, he retouched the cross to make both arms equal length. Later on he even added a waterfall to the picture by printing it in from another negative. As if that wasn't enough, he also tinkered with the shape of an ice pack to the right of the cross to make it look like a "snow angel." In his search for the mountain and his manipulation of the photograph, it's clear that Jackson understood perfectly how valuable the photograph would be. He was right. It became the survey's most popular picture, and copies were a common sight on the walls of homes and churches.

From 1873 until it ended in 1878, the Hayden survey spent most of its time working in the Rocky Mountains in Colorado, an area that was rapidly being developed. Railroads penetrated the wilderness and towns dotted the valleys. When he came upon Silverton, Colorado, in 1874, Jackson remarked in his diary, "as we enter the town we find that it consists of about a dozen new homes–half of them staked off over pretty much the whole valley."[6] But Jackson's photographs from that time give little indication of the pace of settlement. Most of them are mountain views, including the famous Mount of the Holy Cross, in which the land is still pristine wilderness. Jackson studiously avoided traces of human presence, still presenting the West as virgin land ripe with promise. But these photographs have a different feel from the work of the survey's first three years. Now Jackson was not so much discovering new wonders as working familiar ground, more and more using his skills to *create* a vision of a West that was quickly vanishing.

After the Hayden survey ended in 1878, Jackson was kept busy for a time making prints for reports and catalogs. By 1880, his work as a government employee over, Jackson needed to move on to something else. He decided to stake his fortunes on Denver. "I liked the way the place had grown," he wrote, "from a raw town of 5,000, when I first saw it in 1870, to a flourishing city seven times that size. I was sure it would keep on growing and that I should be prosperous there. And I was right on both my guesses."

Jackson first went to New York to meet with railroad magnate Jay Gould to drum up business photographing along several lines that

Gould controlled. Then he headed out to Denver and immediately rented studio space. His aim was to combine studio and outdoor work. "I was still firm in my resolve never to coop myself up indoors again; but I also knew that portrait work was the bread and butter of every photographer. In the summers, when such business was dull, I could work for the railroads and the big picture jobbers–and for my own pleasure. In the winters I would stick to my bench and make money."

With his reputation and connections, Jackson's business was soon flourishing. The Denver & Rio Grande Railroad commissioned him to photograph along its line. The motto of the D&RG was "The Scenic Line of America." Jackson's job was to publicize Colorado as a scenic wonderland–a wonderland that could best be seen from the comfort of a Pullman car. Tourism boomed as the railroads catered to easterners wanting to escape the crowding and dirt and pollution of the cities. The West was becoming a familiar place. It was losing the aura of mystery that had hovered over it before the era of exploration and the arrival of the railroads. The publication of images and travel writing designed to lure tourists was big business by the 1880s, and Jackson was part of it. In large part, the nature of his work during these years was determined by the narrow demands of the publicity industry. His photographs now had to present the West as a tempting vacationland, a wilderness experience without the discomforts of wilderness travel. Jackson's friend, the journalist Ernest Ingersoll, summed it up nicely in his account of a trip through the Rockies called *The Crest of the Continent: A Record of a Summer's Ramble in the Rocky Mountains and Beyond* (1885): "Roughing it, within reasonable grounds, is the marrow of this sort of recreation."[7] The reward, he said, is "everlasting refuges from weariness, anxiety, and strife!"

The W.H. Jackson Photo Company prospered during the 1880s. As usual, Jackson hired someone else to do the portrait work while he criss-crossed the state photographing mountains and waterfalls, mining towns, railroad scenes, and Denver's streets and buildings. Jackson became Colorado's greatest booster. Judging by his photographs,

Colorado was the state that had everything: the perfect combination of unspoiled nature and civilized amenities.

Like most railroad photography in the nineteenth century, Jackson's pictures cast the railroad in a heroic light. The nation's love affair with machinery had not yet been dimmed by such things as pollution and destruction of the environment. America's workshops were turning out one technological marvel after another: voices running through wires, lights going on at the flick of a switch, music springing from a revolving cylinder. It was widely believed that the machine would finally conquer nature and free humanity from the curse of labor.

Nothing symbolized the age of the machine and the advance of civilization more impressively than the railroad. A locomotive is an imposing piece of machinery. The rail line running out to the horizon was the road to the future and the steaming locomotive, massive and powerful, the means of getting there. Jackson's photographs glorified the railroad at the same time as they glorified natural beauty. Few people in those days would have seen any contradiction in this. Several of the pictures he did for the tourist trade show the train stopped at some scenic spot with groups of tourists wandering about enjoying the scenery–a perfect marriage of wilderness and civilization. For Jackson, working for the railroads was a far cry from the years of rugged travel with the Hayden survey. He traveled in luxury, often in a private car complete with darkroom.

In 1892, Jackson took a trip with his old friend Thomas Moran. It would be a return to the sites of their work with Hayden survey, a rediscovery of the West as they had found it twenty years before. It wasn't entirely a pleasure trip; both of them had commissions to fulfill, but they hoped to recover some of the excitement and vigor of the past. They were to be disappointed. Only in the remote mountains of Wyoming did Jackson find what remained of an untouched landscape, and he made some large, powerful views of the terrain. But in Yellowstone, all was changed. With tourists clamoring for position, Kodaks in hand, it was nearly impossible to photograph the famous

Colorado Midland Excursion Train, 11 Mile Cañon (between 1887 and 1900) by William Henry Jackson. This photograph of a tourist train stopped beside the South Platte River is an example of Jackson's later work as a publicist for the railroads. The picture shows men, women and children having an enjoyable time in a picturesque mountain setting. Several people are posing for pictures, and a man with a camera and tripod stands in front of the locomotive. Courtesy Colorado Historical Society, neg. CHS-J2239, William Henry Jackson.

sites as unspoiled wilderness. Some places had been partially destroyed by souvenir seekers chipping away pieces of rock. Jackson's photographs from this trip depict Yellowstone as what it had become–a vacation resort.

~

IN 1886, Frederick Ives, who had invented the photogravure process used by Edward Curtis, developed a method for printing photographs mechanically by using a screen called a half-tone screen. This device breaks the photographic image into a field of tiny black and white dots of different sizes and proximity. The photographic image is projected through the half-tone screen onto a light-sensitive metal plate, which is then inked and used to print copies on a high-speed press. This method is still used today. You can easily see the dot pattern by looking at a newspaper photograph through a magnifying glass.

This invention revolutionized the printing and photographic industries, and it marked the beginning of the age of mass media photojournalism. It meant that the market was flooded with cheap prints and postcards, and no one was buying quality photographs like those produced by the W.H. Jackson Photo Company.

One of the major companies cranking out cheap half-tone prints was the Detroit Publishing Company. This company also held the American license for a process called Photochrome that had been developed in Switzerland. This was a lithographic method for making amazingly realistic color prints from black-and-white photographs. Jackson was not only the best landscape photographer in the country; he was also a shrewd businessman and could see the writing on the wall. By 1897, he had sold all of his negatives to the Detroit Publishing Company and had joined the company as a full partner. He moved to Detroit with his family a year later.

Although Jackson continued to photograph, most of his time with the Detroit Publishing Company was spent in administrative work. He oversaw the management of the company's entire stock of photographs, which by 1902 had reached seven million. He was eighty-one years old when he left the company in 1924. He had accomplished a great deal, but he was far from finished. He would live until the age of ninety-nine, still active. In the last years he turned to painting, writing and lecturing. In 1929, he was named research secretary of the Oregon Trail Memorial Association. It was a position that took him west during the summers to lecture to local historical societies and appear at conventions and holiday celebrations. He had become the Grand Old Man, a remnant of a time long gone.

Jackson's work traces the changes in the western landscape during the time of its greatest transformation–from the opening of the transcontinental railroad to the closing of the frontier. He witnessed and participated in the exploration, the settlement, and the commercialization of the West. But at the same time as his pictures document the transformation of the landscape, they also reveal the transformation of white America's attitudes toward it. They tell us how people learned to see the land, and William Henry Jackson's photographs played no small part in teaching them what to see and how to see it.

AFTERWORD

THE FRONTIER PHOTOGRAPHERS helped to create for Americans a West of the imagination, one that promised the best of two worlds—an untouched Eden and an empire ready and waiting for exploitation. Today, there is widespread doubt that we can have it both ways. While parts of the earlier vision have endured, other parts of it have come under more critical scrutiny.

From the beginning of outdoor photography in America, the celebration of wild nature has been its leading theme. Coffee table books and magazines swell with lush images (mostly in color now) of every imaginable mood and gesture nature has to offer. In spite of summer traffic jams in the national parks, or the sprawl and smog of Los Angeles, the West is often still thought of as wilderness, the place where a person can escape the crush of civilization and get back to nature.

This persistent vision of the western landscape made the reputation of America's best-known photographer of the twentieth century, Ansel Adams. The pictures that brought him fame are the magnificent black and white prints of pristine nature, especially of Yosemite, where a hundred years earlier Carleton Watkins had lugged his mammoth cameras. The photographs in Adams's exhibits and books and calendars and postcards are free of the slightest trace of human presence. Although, like Watkins and the others, Adams lent his vision to commercial photography as well, this is the work that was most important to him, and in it the western landscape continues to be a place of spiritual renewal. In a talk to a wilderness conference in 1961, Adams said:

> The stabilization of our [American] society has brought us to the point where we need no longer fight the wild environment. . . .We may approach wilderness environment as a source of physical and mental health, of inspiration, and of the revelation of the greater cosmos of which we are a part.[1]

Without having to "fight the wild environment," Adams and the hundreds who followed him could seek out the beautiful and sublime in nature. The wilderness had become art, and they wanted their photographs to transport us, elevate us, lift us out of ourselves.

But others have viewed the western landscape differently, focusing more sharply, and critically, on the relationship between the land and the people who live on it. When the early photographers included evidence of human presence in their pictures, they usually did it without any sense of intrusion or irony. A locomotive was a welcome sign of advancing civilization. But as the West was filled up and fenced off, that view became harder to hold onto. In 1975 an influential exhibition called *New Topographics* displayed the work of a group of young photographers for whom the relationship between the land and the people is uneasy at best. The work of Robert Adams, Lewis Baltz, and Nicholas Nixon, to name a few, shows us a landscape altered and scarred by human occupation, marked by power lines, tract houses, and chainlink fences. These photographers avoid the beautiful and the dramatic. They see instead the banal and the downright ugly—the sad footprint of human occupation. For them the West is Eden despoiled.

As opposite as nature photography and New Topographics appear at first glance, they both hark back to the American dream of the West as garden of the world. One shows us what's left of Eden, and the other what has happened to it. Behind both of them lies the ideal of the grand empty vistas of the early photographers, the ones who first gave shape and substance to the vision.

The vision of the frontier photographers is even more apparent in the work inspired by the photographer/geologist Mark Klett. In 1977, Klett established the Rephotographic Survey Project, the purpose of which was to find the sites documented by the photographers of the nineteenth century surveys and to photograph them from exactly the same point of view. This freezes time, and allows us to see exactly how the landscape has changed. But it expresses time, not a new sensibility about the West. Perhaps after all, the photograph that is produced with today's high-tech, portable equipment will remain forever indebted to that first photographer, who pushed his way to the top of the hill with his mules, planted his feet, treated his plates, hoped everything would stay still long enough for him to take a picture, and created, instead, a vision.

NOTES

Introduction: Picturing the West

1. Daniel J. Boorstin, *The Americans: The National Experience* (New York: Random House, 1965), p. 228.

2. Ibid., p. 225.

3. Ibid., p. 229.

4. William E. Connelley, *A Standard History of Kansas and Kansans*, 1998, chapter 7. Internet. KS GenWeb Archives. 169.147.169.151/genweb/archives/index.html

5. Henry Nash Smith, *Virgin Land: The American West as Symbol and Myth* (Cambridge, Mass.: Harvard University Press, 1950), p. 179.

6. Boorstin, p. 232.

7. Smith, p. 123.

Chapter 2: Going West: The First Wave

1. Robert Taft, *Photography and the American Scene: A Social History, 1839-1889* (New York: Dover Publications, 1938), p. 262.

2. Carvalho, Solomon N. *Incidents of Travel and Adventure in the Far West*, chapter 11. Internet. www.jewish-history.com/wildwest/carvalho.

3. Ibid.

4. Ibid.

5. Ibid., chapter 13.

6. Quoted in Taft, p. 264.

7. Mary Warner Marien, "Imagining the Corporate Sublime," in *Carleton Watkins: Selected Texts and Bibliography*, ed. Amy Rule (Oxford, England: CLIO Press, 1993), p. 9.

8. Carleton Watkins, quoted in Peter E. Palmquist, *Carleton Watkins: Photographer of the American West* (Albuquerque: University of New Mexico Press, 1983), p. 72.

Chapter 3: Imagining America

1. Robert Hughes, *American Visions: The Epic History of Art in America* (New York: Alfred A. Knopf, 1997), p. 138.
2. William Cullen Bryant, "Forest Hymn," Internet. www.bartleby.com
3. Boorstin, *The Americans*, p. 268.
4. Ibid., p. 266.

Chapter 4: War Photographers and Western Journeys

1. John Samson, "Photographs from the High Rockies," *Harper's New Monthly Magazine*, Vol. 39, no. 232 (New York: Harper Brothers, Sept. 1869), p. 467. Internet, Cornell University Library. www.cdl.library.cornell.edu/moa
2. Ibid., p. 471.

Chapter 5: Photographers of the Local Scene

1. Taft, *Photography*, p. 138.
2. William Henry Jackson, *Time Exposure* (New York: G.P. Putnam's Sons, 1940), p. 173.
3. Mark H. Brown and W.R. Felton, *Before Barbed Wire* (New York: Henry Holt and Co., 1956), p. 19.
4. Ibid., p. 26.
5. Ibid., p. 219.
6. Ibid., p. 30.
7. Quoted in Mark H. Brown and W.R. Felton, *The Frontier Years: L.A. Huffman, Photographer of the Plains* (New York: Henry Holt and Co., 1955), p. 52.
8. Brown and Felton, *Before Barbed Wire*, p. 12.
9. Brown and Felton, *The Frontier Years*, p. 26.
10. John Carter, *Solomon D. Butcher: Photographing the American Dream* (Lincoln: University of Nebraska Press, 1985), p. 2.
11. Ibid., p. 3.
12. Ibid., p. 5.
13. Jackson, p. 26.
14. Carter, p. 13.
15. Ibid., p. 9.

Chapter 6: The Many Faces of the American Indian

1. William H. Goetzmann, *Exploration and Empire: The Explorer and Scientist in the Winning of the American West* (New York: Alfred A. Knopf, 1966), pp. 328-29.

2. Paula Richardson Fleming and Judith Luskey, *The North American Indians in Early Photographs* (New York: Dorset Press, 1986), p. 22.

3. Goetzmann, pp. 523-24.

4. Horace Poley, letter to Elsie Beachtold, February 20, 1935. Horace S. Poley online exhibit, Denver Public Library, www.gowest.coalliance.org.

5. Adam Clark Vroman, *Photo Era*, VI, 1901, pp. 269-70. Quoted in *Adam Clark Vroman, Photographer of the Southwest*, ed. Ruth I. Mahood (Los Angeles: The Ward Ritchie Press, 1961), p. 13.

Chapter 7: Saving Shadows: The Indian Photography of Edward S. Curtis

1. Edward S. Curtis, *The North American Indian*. Quoted in Rod Slemmons, catalog essay for the exhibition, *Shadowy Evidence: The Photography of Edward S. Curtis and His Contemporaries* (Seattle: Seattle Art Museum, 1989), Internet. www.faculty.washington.edu.

Chapter 8: The Last of the Great Frontier Photographers

1. William Henry Jackson, *Time Exposure*, p. 81. [Unless otherwise noted, all quotations from Jackson in this chapter are from this book].

2. Ferdinand Hayden, *Fourth Annual Report* (Washington, D.C., 1870), p. 37. Quoted in Peter Hales, *William Henry Jackson and the Transformation of the American Landscape* (Philadelphia, Pa.: Temple University Press, 1988), p. 73.

3. Ibid., p. 34.

4. Thomas Moran, quoted in Thurman Wilkins, *Thomas Moran, Artist of the Mountains* (Norman: University of Oklahoma Press, 1966), p. 6.

5. Ibid.

6. Jackson, quoted in Hales, p. 113.

7. Ernest Ingersoll, *The Crest of the Continent*, quoted in Hales, p. 144.

Afterword

1. David Brower, ed. *Wilderness: America's Living Heritage* (San Francisco: The Sierra Club, 1961) p. 52.

BIBLIOGRAPHY

Andrews, Ralph W. *Photographers of the Frontier West: Their Lives and Their Works*. Seattle: Superior Publishing Company, 1965.

Beverly, Robert. *The History and Present State of Virginia* (1705). Ed. Louis B. Wright. Chapel Hill: University of North Carolina Press, 1947.

Boorstin, Daniel J. *The Americans: The National Experience*. New York: Random House, 1965.

Brown, Mark H. and Felton, W.R. *Before Barbed Wire*. New York: Henry Holt and Co., 1956.

——. *The Frontier Years: L.A. Huffman, Photographer of the Plains*. New York: Henry Holt and Co., 1956.

Bryant, William Cullen, "Forest Hymn" in *Bartleby Verse: English and American Poetry: 1250–1920*, Vol. II. New York: New American Library, 1999. (Internet. www.bartleby.com/verse)

Carter, John. *Solomon D. Butcher: Photographing the American Dream*. Lincoln: University of Nebraska Press, 1985.

Brower, David, ed. *Wilderness: America's Living Heritage*. San Francisco: The Sierra Club, 1961.

Fleming, Paula Richardson and Luskey, Judith. *The North American Indians in Early Photographs*. New York: Dorset Press, 1986.

Gardner, Alexander. *Gardner's Photographic Sketch Book of the Civil War*. New York: Dover Publications, 1959.

Goetzmann, William H. *Exploration and Empire: The Explorer and Scientist in the Winning of the American West*. New York: Alfred A. Knopf, 1966.

Hales, Peter B. *William Henry Jackson and the Transformation of the American Landscape*. Philadelphia, Pa.: Temple University Press, 1988.

Hoobler, Dorothy and Thomas. *Photographing the Frontier.* New York: G.P. Putnam's Sons, 1980.

Hughes, Robert. *American Visions: The Epic History of Art in America*. New York: Alfred A. Knopf, 1997.

Jackson, Clarence S. *Picture Maker of the Old West: William Henry Jackson.* New York: Charles Scribner's Sons, 1947.

Jackson, William Henry. *Time Exposure*. New York: G.P. Putnam's Sons, 1940.

Jones, William C. and Elizabeth. *William Henry Jackson's Colorado*. Boulder, Colo.: Pruett Publishing Co., 1975.

Lawlor, Laurie. *Window on the West: The Frontier Photography of William Henry Jackson*. New York: Holiday House, 1999.

———. *Shadow Catcher: The Life and Work of Edward S. Curtis*. New York: Walker and Company, 1994.

Marien, Mary Warner, "Imagining the Corporate Sublime," in *Carleton Watkins: Selected Texts and Bibliography*, ed. Amy Rule. Oxford, England: CLIO Press, 1993.

Naef, Weston. *Era of Exploration: Landscape Photography in the American West, 1860-1885*. New York: Albright-Knox Art Gallery and The Metropolitan Museum of Art, 1975.

Newhall, Beaumont. *The History of Photography*. New York: The Museum of Modern Art, 1964.

Palmquist, Peter E. *Carleton Watkins: Photographer of the American West*. Albuquerque: University of New Mexico Press, 1983.

Samson, John, "Photographs from the High Rockies," in *Harper's New Monthly Magazine*, Vol. 34, no. 232. New York: Harper

Brothers, Sept. 1869. Internet, Cornell University Library. www.cdl.library.cornell.edu

Smith, Henry Nash. *Virgin Land: The American West as Symbol and Myth.* Cambridge, Mass.: Harvard University Press, 1950.

Taft, Robert. *Photography and the American Scene: A Social History, 1839–1889.* New York: Dover Publications, 1938.

Vroman, Adam Clark. *Photographer of the Southwest.* Ed. Ruth I. Mahood. Los Angeles: The Ward Ritchie Press, 1961.

Webb, William and Weinstein, Robert A. *Dwellers at the Source.* New York: Grossman Publishers, 1973.

Wilkins, Thurman. *Thomas Moran, Artist of the Mountains.* Norman: University of Oklahoma Press, 1966.

WEBOGRAPHY

THERE ARE MANY sources of information on the internet for topics covered in this book, as well as several good digitized collections of nineteenth-century western photographs. Photographs in these collections can be viewed on the Internet. The ones listed here are the best I have found.

The largest general collections of photographs are at the Library of Congress's Prints and Photographs division, the George Eastman House, and a website maintained jointly by the Denver Public Library, the Colorado Historical Society, and the Denver Art Museum.

The Library of Congress website (www.loc.gov) has a large digitized database of prints and photographs. Of special interest for the work of photographers in this book are the following exhibits in the library's American Memory collection: *Curtis, Edward~North American Indian Photographs~Ca. 1900; Prairie Settlement, Nebraska~Photographs and Letters~1862-1912* (includes 500 Solomon Butcher photographs); *Western U.S.~Photographs~1860-1920* (photographs from the collection of the Denver Public Library); *Utah and Western Migration~Multiformat~1846-69;* and *Great Plains~Photographs~1880–1920.* These sites also contain biographical information, essays, and other documents relevant to the photographs. The American Memory exhibit called *The Evolution of the Conservation*

Movement, 1850-1920 also has a selection of Thomas Moran's paintings, including *The Grand Canyon of the Yellowstone.*

In addition to these collections, you can also search the database by the photographer's name. There are sizeable collections by Carleton Watkins, Timothy O'Sullivan (many of them Civil War photos), Mathew Brady (portraits and Civil War photos), and William Henry Jackson. The collection also houses the one existing daguerreotype by Solomon Carvalho.

The Denver Public Library's site (www.gowest.coalliance.org) has a large digitized database and a gallery featuring several special displays, including selections from the work of David Barry and Horace Poley, including the exhibit noted in chapter 6. The search feature allows browsing by photographer, subject, or title. The largest collection in the database consists of over 6,600 photographs by William Henry Jackson. Since there are so many, and a search of Jackson's name brings up the whole collection in random order, it's best to limit your search by putting a slash and a specific topic after the name. For example, Jackson, William Henry/ railroads, or /Rocky Mountains, or /mining towns.

This website also contains smaller collections by Timothy O'Sullivan, John K. Hillers, Carleton Watkins, and many lesser-known photographers. Other ways of searching include browsing by name (e.g. Sitting Bull) or subject (e.g. silver mining). Lists of photographers and subjects in the database are also available.

George Eastman House International Museum of Photography and Film (www.eastman.org) has a fine online exhibit of western photographs that includes collections on the King and the Wheeler surveys. From the home page, follow links to *Photography Collections on Line*, then to *Still Photography Collections-by Subject*, and finally to *American West Collections.* All of the photographs from the Clarence King survey of the fortieth parallel are by Timothy O'Sullivan. The Wheeler survey pictures are by O'Sullivan and William Bell. Also at this site is the Henry Gannett Album of William Henry Jackson photographs. All of these exhibits can be viewed as pages of thumbnails that can be individually enlarged. An index with the name of the photographer and the title of each photograph is also provided.

There is also an extensive Civil War collection here, including Alexander Gardner's *Photographic Sketch Book of the Civil War*. This site also contains a series by Carleton Watkins. More photographs by Watkins can be seen at the Yosemite National Park website (www.yosemite.ca.us) and at a site maintained by the Watkins family (www.watkins.org).

The Getty Museum of Los Angeles, California (www.getty.edu) has short features on artists and photographers. Here you will find information and a few examples of work by Mathew Brady, Edward Curtis, Alexander Gardner, William Henry Jackson, Timothy O'Sullivan, A.J. Russell, Adam Clark Vroman, and Carleton Watkins. The Getty site also has a number of short features on photography, including nineteenth century prints such as stereographs, card photographs (*cartes de visite*) and daguerreotypes, albumen, and photogravure.

The California Museum of Photography at the University of California at Riverside (www.cmp.ucr.edu) has a website with an extensive collection of Adam Clark Vroman's photographs of Southwest Indians.

The complete text of Solomon Carvalho's *Incidents of Travel and Adventure in the Far West* resides at www.jewish-history.com. Click on "Jews in the Wild West."

The Nebraska Historical Society (www.nebraskahistory.org) has an exhibit titled *Solomon D. Butcher: Photographs of the Nebraska Homestead Experience*. The site includes a biography of Butcher and a selection of photographs with commentary.

The National Gallery of Art (www.nga.gov) has a small collection of Carleton Watkins photographs, a brief biography, and an informative essay written in connection with the 1999 exhibit *Carleton Watkins: The Art of Perception*. Also at this site is a feature on Thomas Moran that traces his career from 1837 to 1926. Another useful essay on Moran, with pictures, can be found at the website of the American Studies Department at the University of Virginia (www.xroads.virginia.edu).

Traditional Fine Art On Line (www.tfaoi.com) provides links to a number of photographers under its American Photography heading, including Edward Curtis and Carleton Watkins. This site also features a variety of nineteenth-century American landscape painters, including Sanford Gifford, Thomas Moran, and Albert Bierstadt.

The Public Broadcasting System website (www.pbs.org) presents an online mutimedia tour of its eight-part television documentary series *The West*, which includes images, background material, and links to other sources.

Treasurenet (www.treasurenet.com) offers an interesting assortment of Civil War and western photographs, categorized according to subject: Surveys and Expeditions, The Law of the West, Towns of Dust and Rock, and so on.

Both the Central Pacific and Union Pacific railroad websites have large collections of photographs taken by the men who worked for the railroads. These collections naturally feature pictures having to do with railroads–trains, bridges, stations, etc.–but also include scenery and town views. The Central Pacific's photographic history museum is at www.cprr.org This site also contains a wide variety of documents and miscellaneous articles related to the railroad, photography, and western history. A link to the Union Pacific photo gallery can be found at www.up.com/aboutup/history.

A history of the four great western surveys of the 1860s and 70s can be found at the United States Geological Survey website (www.usgs.gov). Look for Circular 1050, *The United States Geological Survey. 1879-1989* (in spite of the dates, this is a complete history from the beginning of government surveys in the early 1800s).

INDEX